SPEAKING OF GOD

Speaking of God

THE NATURE AND PURPOSE OF THEOLOGICAL LANGUAGE

BY WILLIAM HORDERN

Wipf and Stock Publishers
EUGENE, OREGON

Wipf and Stock Publishers
199 West 8th Avenue, Suite 3
Eugene, Oregon 97401

Speaking of God
The Nature and Purpose of Theological Language
By Hordern, William E.

ISBN: 1-57910-974-8
Publication date: May, 2002
Previously published by Macmillan Company, 1964.

TO JOYCE

PREFACE

When I took my first teaching position as a member of the Philosophy and Religion Department of Swarthmore College, I was thrust into the midst of analytical philosophers. It was an experience for which my theological education had not prepared me, and I fear that my philosophical colleagues found me a rather stubborn learner. But I did learn from them. In the process I became convinced that a major task for theology today is to converse with this philosophy. Wherever I have spoken with those who face the student generation of our time I have found a similar conviction. There has been a considerable flow of books on the subject in recent years, but even so the conversation has been no more than opened.

The tragedy of the relation between theology and philosophy since the rise of analytical philosophy has been that there has been no real conversation between the two disciplines. Most of the books that have dealt with analytical philosophy and theology have been written from one side and have been attempts to annihilate the other side. I happen to hold the still rather unorthodox opinion that the two disciplines can be mutually stimulating friends. Thus I call my book a "conversation." This is somewhat presumptuous, since I am not a philosophical expert and this turns out to be my report of the conversation. As with all reports of conversations, the other party may want to complain, "That's not quite what I meant." But this is not so unfortunate in light of the fact that I see this book as a beginning and not as a final or definitive statement. Perhaps it can serve to introduce theologians to philosophers and stimulate others to converse.

I owe many debts for whatever merits the book may have. Besides the help I received from my former colleagues at Swarthmore, I have learned much through discussion with my present colleagues at Garrett Theological Seminary, particularly Philip Watson, Tyler Thompson, and Samuel Laeuchli. The late Willem Zuurdeeg, of McCormick Theological Seminary, was of great assistance at the beginning of my labors. I deeply regret that his untimely death prevented his seeing the final manuscript. Jules Moreau, of Seabury-Western Theological Seminary, has been a continual inspiration through his writings and personal conversation. The students at Garrett who took my course on this subject have been of inestimable help. If this book differs significantly from what I stated in class, this is in large part because of what I learned from them. I should like to mention the help of one student in particular—Ronald Goetz, my advisee in the doctoral program—who acted as a sounding board and critic for my ideas on many occasions.

I want to thank Garrett Theological Seminary for the sabbatical leave that enabled me to complete this work.

Last, and my no means least, I extend my gratitude to my wife for her help on correcting the manuscript and for her sublime patience with the mess in my study while it was being written.

CONTENTS

INTRODUCTION

In their musical *Flower Drum Song* Rodgers and Hammerstein have a song that gaily asks, "How will we ever communicate without communication?" The satire is timely because our age is fascinated by communication. Modern advertising has become a major industry that is preoccupied with communicating to potential buyers. The first question that political parties ask about their programs and candidates is "Can they communicate with the voter?" Modern education is preoccupied with problems of teacher-pupil communication. Modern philosophers have come close to reducing philosophy to the analysis of language, the basic tool of communication. Whenever one picks up a modern book on theology he is almost certain to find some reference to communication.

This preoccupation with communication is ironical, for we are living in the age of miracles in this realm. We have watched the perfecting of the means of communication until we can dial telephone numbers to speak to someone thousands of miles away. Through "Telstar" we can watch and hear men on the other side of the earth. Yet, in the midst of these miracles, many have stopped to recall what Henry Thoreau said when he heard of the proposed construction of a magnetic telegraph between Maine and Texas: " . . . but Maine and Texas, it may be, have nothing important to communicate." We are beginning to see that new means of communication are mere curiosities unless we have something to say. Worse still, means of communication may stifle communication. For example, it is often charged that television is killing the art of conversation. The age in which it has become simple to speak to or listen to millions around the world is also the age in which real communication between persons is more often a nostalgic dream than a reality.

Our age is symbolized by the Biblical story of the Tower of Babel (Gen. 11:1–9). In the beginning, it tells us, "the whole earth had one language and few words." Then men decided to build a tower to the heavens that would make them equal to God. To prevent this, God confused their language so that they could not understand one another's speech. The Tower of Babel is a symbol of our time, for we are in an age that no longer has "one language and few words." We have many languages, and our words are so elastic in meaning that we can no longer understand one another.

This lack of understanding takes many forms. Although physically we have become "one world," politically we are tragically and dangerously divided. And the political division involves a problem of language. Everyone is for "peace," "freedom," and "democracy," but these noble words vary in meaning with the user, so that we dare not agree with a proposition until we know who said it. Members of the same university faculty cannot speak to one another if they leave humdrum affairs and approach their specialities. A congressman recently protested, after listening to a briefing delivered to his committee by a group of scientists, that he could understand nothing that they had said, and yet on the basis of their testimony he was supposed to legislate responsibly. A recent survey showed that the lower-income groups are being denied adequate psychiatric care, not so much because of economic poverty as because of the inability of psychiatrist and patient to understand each other when they are divided by class lines.[1] A common complaint against our poets and artists, who presumably are masters of communication, is that few can understand them. In such an age it comes as no surprise to find that not only laymen but also clergymen complain that they cannot understand modern theologians.

In the Tower of Babel story the confusion of language was primarily the result of sin. Presumptuous men, trying to usurp God's place, were thrown into a confusion of voices to disrupt their nefarious plans. The modern breakdown in communication is not simply a result of sin. As our examples have shown, it is due partly to the fact that we no longer have "one language and few words." The growth of knowledge has given birth to a host of technical jargons. But sin is not absent. Communication fails not only because our jargons differ but also because we seek to increase our prestige by keeping our special knowledge and its jargon as esoteric as possible. One of the primary motivations behind the invention of more efficient means of communication is the desire to control the actions of others by means of advertising, propaganda, and "education." Communication is disrupted not only by our "many words," it is disrupted by our sinful use of language to mislead, control, and exploit our fellowmen.

The Christian faith has an obvious concern with communication. It rests upon the belief that God speaks and calls man into fellowship. The Christian Church is endowed with good news to tell, a Gospel to proclaim. If it cannot communicate its good news, it will fail in its primary purpose.

There are many levels at which the problem of Christian communication is raised. The preacher is concerned with the structure of sermons that communicate. The pastoral counselor is concerned with methods of counseling that will make therapeutic communication possible. The religious educator studies the characteristics of each age level to learn how he may communicate with his pupils. The Biblical scholar seeks to translate the ancient manuscripts into modern tongues so that the original meaning is both retained and made understandable. Others are concerned with questions of how radio, the arts, television, and literature may be used in communicating the Gospel. In recent years we have heard much about "nonverbal" means of communication, which reminds us that communication is not limited to speech.

But central to all problems of Christian communication is a theological concern. This is the question of how we can use human means, be they words or acts, to speak of the God who created the heavens and the earth. If God is the Creator and not a creature, if God is not a thing in the world but the Lord over it, how can we take words that we have coined to speak about creaturely things and use these earthbound tools to speak about the transcendent God? Christian theology always has been aware of this problem, but in the modern world the problem has arisen in a new fashion. The contemporary problem is revealed by the degree to which our classic expressions of the faith have become a paradoxical mixture of asset and liability.

The Bible, the historic creeds, and the traditional theological convictions are still rocks of strength upon which the Christian builds. They give him a sense of unity with the Christian past and a direction for the future. One often feels the thrill that runs through a congregation as it rises to its feet to proclaim with the Church of the ages, "I believe in God, the Father Almighty . . ." Far from losing these foundations of the faith, modern Christians have been rediscovering the treasures of their past. Even Christians who would not sing with gusto "Give Me That Old-Time Religion" do unite in singing "Faith of Our Fathers, Living Still." In short, there is power in Christian language that still sustains the Church.

But the paradox appears because this historic Christian language is also an embarrassment. The Christian is aware that his classical terms and thought forms are often an offense and scandal to the modern world. The New Testament warns us that the Gospel will be a stumbling block to the natural man (I Cor. 1:23). But today we have the uncomfortable feeling that we are giving the wrong offense. Modern man is not simply shocked at the Gospel: he is often so alienated by the language forms in which it comes that he does not even hear the Gospel.

We see many symptoms of this embarrassment. No matter how fervently on Sunday morning the Christian repeats phrases like "Born of the Virgin Mary," "the Resurrection of the body," or "Descended into hell," he seldom allows such terminology to creep into his after-dinner conversation, his business affairs, or his cocktail hours. He does not do so because he senses that such terms sound quaint, faintly humorous, and ridiculous in the modern world. The average minister uses one set of phrases and terms from the pulpit and another set of phrases in personal conversation even with those who hear him every Sunday. And if he does not have a different way of expressing himself, his people are likely to complain that he "preaches at them" even during a friendly visit.

The problem of language often comes into the open when a young man is entering the Christian ministry. If he belongs to a denomination that requires adherence to a creedal statement, he may have considerable heart searching. He cannot agree completely with the creed, yet he feels in essential harmony with the aims and purposes of his church. He is convinced that he is called of God to serve in its ministry. What does he do? Often he accepts the creed with no hesitation and, if challenged in private, will say, "Oh, I took that phrase symbolically." But what does this mean? Is this a theological way of crossing one's fingers while telling a lie? Or is it a mature doctrine of symbolism? If it is a symbol, what kind of symbol is it?

The fundamentalist-liberal controversy early in this century arose primarily out of the problem of communicating the classical faith in the modern world. Christian liberalism was determined to remove all unnecessary scandal from Christian thought. It was confident that the solid kernel of truth in Christianity could be preserved while discarding the chaff of outworn concepts. Liberals thus tried to sort out the "abiding truths" from the "changing categories." Among the changing categories discarded were miracle stories, the second coming of Christ, original sin, and the inerrancy of the Bible. On the other hand, liberalism welcomed the discoveries and theories of modern science, including the theory of evolution and the findings of Biblical criticism.

With the rise of liberalism many Christians became alarmed that the baby was being thrown out with the bath. They rallied under the banner of fundamentalism to defend the historic faith. The fundamentalists placed their faith in the inerrancy of the Bible as the God-given record of God's own way of salvation. The miracles, so offensive to the modern mind, were firmly held as evidence that the Supernatural God had entered into his world with his creative power. The original sin of man and salvation through the vicarious atonement of Christ were held to be central to the Gospel. The fundamentalist often opposed science and Biblical criticism.

By the end of the twenties the liberal cause was in the ascendancy, whereas the fundamentalists were losing ground in the major denominations. But in the hour of its triumph liberalism found a new theological mood arising. This new theology, often called "neoorthodoxy," was really a series of theological movements. Its essence was a return to historical and Biblical Christianity without becoming fundamentalist. It seemed that it had transcended the old theological quarrels. It did not enter into battle with science or Biblical scholarship. But doctrines like the fall of man, original sin, and the second coming of Christ, which often had been tossed out the front door by liberalism, were now restored through the back door by the neoorthodox as profound "myths" or "symbols." Neoorthodoxy charged that neither the fundamentalist who accepted these doctrines nor the liberal who rejected them had been able to see past their literal meaning to their profound truth about the God-man relationship. But, understood as myths or as symbols, they could still speak to the condition of modern man without insulting his intelligence.

The problem of how historic Christianity could be made meaningful to modern man was by no means solved by neoorthodoxy. It began to appear in a multitude of new forms. It became obvious that, while theology had increased the subtlety of its thought, it had left most laymen and often the average clergyman in the dark. Such people asked: What is left after all the discussion of myth, symbol, paradox, and demythologization? Does the theologian still mean what Christians have meant through the centuries, or has he turned his back on the faith? Has Christian language become merely poetry to express philosophical, ethical, or existential concerns?

One of the chief complaints against the liberal during the heyday of liberalism was that it was easy to find out what he did not believe but often difficult to find out what he did believe. At first sight it did not seem that this criticism could be made of the neoorthodox. He reaffirmed many of the cornerstones of faith rejected by the liberals. But to the layman it still often seemed easier to find out what the theologian did not believe.

The layman heard the theologian say that he believed in God but could not say that God exists. He believed in creation but did not suppose that this tells us anything about the origin of the universe as science discusses it. He accepted the doctrine of the Virgin Birth, but he did not suppose that this is information about the biological origin of Jesus. He believed in the resurrection of the body but did not suppose that this meant anything so crude as that our physical body will live after death. He believed in eternal life, but this does not imply an everlasting life for persons. He believed in Christ's second coming but did not suppose that this meant that Jesus was going to reappear in our midst. He believed in the fall of man but did not believe that a historical Adam and Eve once lived in the Garden of Eden. When the liberal said that he did not believe a doctrine, he meant what the layman meant, and they could argue the point. But when a theologian says that he believes in the Resurrection of Christ but does not consider that the Gospel stories of the Resurrection are history, the layman has a feeling that theological wool is being pulled over his eyes.

What does it mean to the layman when he hears Biblical stories or Christian doctrines described as "myths"? President John Kennedy, in his 1962 Commencement Address at Yale, said, "The great enemy of truth is very often not the lie—deliberate, contrived, and dishonest, but the myth—persistent, persuasive, and unrealistic." Laymen immediately understood Kennedy's use of "myth." But when the theologian says that the Bible contains many myths, will not the layman assume that he is saying that the Bible is "persistent, persuasive, and unrealistic"?

If the theologian says that theological statements are symbolic, this also disturbs the layman. If something is a symbol it seems to be less real, less meaningful, and less important than nonsymbolic statements. That religious language must be symbolic is, in one sense, axiomatic. Words are symbols that stand for or point to certain realities or activities. But obviously when a theologian argues that theological language is symbolic, he is trying to say something more than that it is symbolic because it is language.

When the theologian argues that he accepts Scripture or doctrine as symbols, he seems to be using the second meaning of symbol given by the *Shorter Oxford English Dictionary:* "Something that stands for, represents, or denotes something else (not by exact resemblance, but by vague suggestion, or by some accidental or conventional relation)." As such the meaning of "symbol" seems fairly clear. Normally we use words in what Aquinas called their "univocal" sense; that is, in different contexts the same word means the same thing. Thus, if one says that a cow is lean and a man is lean, the word "lean" is used univocally to describe both creatures as being under the normal weight for their species. On the other hand, when Shakespeare has Caesar say, "Yond Cassius has a lean and hungry look," he is obviously speaking symbolically. Used univocally, this sentence would simply state that Cassius looked underweight and in need of a square meal. But leanness and hunger have become symbolic of certain ominous qualities in the character of Cassius. In symbolism a statement, story, or thing takes on meaning beyond its normal univocal implications. All this is a quite normal use of language, and the theologian should have no difficulty in defending his use of symbolism. But the problem is to decide what the theologian is symbolizing.

When we speak symbolically in terms of Cassius' "lean and hungry look," the symbols are meaningful because, if pressed, we would be able to translate what we have in mind into univocal language. Such translation would lose an important, if indefinable, element that is in Shakespeare's statement, but it could convey the basic meaning. The problem of modern theology is that it has often been unable to state clearly what is being symbolized by the theological symbols.

The general problem of the use of symbols in theology is illustrated in the work of Tillich. Early in his career Tillich accepted the point made by Wilbur Urban that if we are to speak of symbolic knowledge, we must delimit the realm referred to symbolically by a nonsymbolic statement.[2] That is, if everything we say about something is symbolic, how can we know to what the symbols point?

To meet Urban's point Tillich, in the first volume of his *Systematic Theology*, emphasized that the only nonsymbolic statement we could make about God is that "God is being itself."[3] This statement served as a nonsymbolic statement to which the symbolic statements could point. But no aspect of Tillich's thought received more criticism than this reference to God as "being itself." Many argued that it is itself a purely symbolic statement. Others argued that "being itself" is not the Christian God. Walter Kaufmann sums up the critique by saying, "But this is surely neither a symbolic statement nor a nonsymbolic statement: it is no statement at all, it is a definition—and as it happens, a definition utterly at odds with the meaning of 'God' in probably more than 95 per cent of our religious tradition."[4]

Apparently Tillich was persuaded by the criticism, for in the second volume of his work he tells us that the only nonsymbolic statement we can make about God is "the statement that everything we say about God is symbolic."[5] Critics, however, were quick to point out that this is not a statement about God but a statement about statements about God. In the same paragraph Tillich argues that statements such as "God is being itself" are on the "boundary line at which symbolic and nonsymbolic coincide." Having conceded that all his statements about God are symbolic, or on the boundary line between symbolic and nonsymbolic, can Tillich meet Urban's point? Can we know to what Tillich's symbols refer?

Tillich tries to avoid an impasse by his distinction between signs and symbols. Signs, he says, only point to some reality and are quite arbitrary; they can be changed at will. Thus a red light becomes a sign for stopping, but it could be changed, for it has no essential relation to stopping.[6] But a symbol, declares Tillich, "participates" in that to which it points. Therefore, although symbols may grow or die, they cannot be invented or changed at will.[7] Religious symbols express man's ultimate concern. It is senseless to discuss the existence or nonexistence of God because "It is meaningless to question the ultimacy of an ultimate concern. This element in the idea of God is in itself certain. The symbolic expression of this element varies endlessly through the whole history of mankind."[8]

But still there are difficulties. Tillich's distinction between sign and symbol does not correspond to any normal usage of the words. This is not an insurmountable obstacle, but it militates against the communication of his meaning.

More important, it is difficult to see what it means for a symbol to participate in that which it symbolizes. Tillich can say, "A religious symbol *is* true if it adequately expresses the correlation of some person with final revelation. A religious symbol can die only if the correlation of which it is an adequate expression dies."[9] But, as George Tavard argues, if a symbol ever has been truly a symbol of God, how can it die or cease to be a symbol?[10] Does its truth depend upon man's reaction to it? Tillich does seem to think that there is a truth to symbols apart from the reaction of men. He can say that the real problem is "which of the innumerable symbols of faith is most adequate to the meaning of faith."[11] This seems to imply that something more than the correlation of the person with final revelation is involved in the life and death of symbols.

Because of such inherent vagueness in Tillich's use of the term "symbol" we find that persons of widely different convictions can agree with him. Many traditional Christians quote Tillich with approval. On the other hand, J. H. Randall, Jr., in writing a defense of naturalistic humanism can claim that he is theologically closest to Tillich.[12] Both sides cannot be correct in claiming Tillich as their own, but which side is correct is difficult to see in light of the obscurities of Tillich's use of symbols.

While Tillich has been reinterpreting theological language in terms of symbols, Bultmann and his school have been concerned to "demythologize" the Gospel message. On the one hand, argues Bultmann, the scientific world view of modern man makes it impossible to accept the mythical language of the Bible.[13] But, on the other hand, insists Bultmann, the mythical language is itself inappropriate to the Gospel. The purpose of myth is to express man's belief that the origin and purpose of his world are not to be found within it but beyond it. Myth uses the imagery of this world to describe that which transcends the world, so that its purpose is negated by its choice of terms.[14] Consequently Bultmann does not want to abandon the New Testament mythology but wants to "demythologize" it, that is, to translate it into existential terms.

In his last lonely days in prison Dietrich Bonhoeffer became haunted with the conviction that if Christians were to communicate with the modern world, they needed a radical revision of their language.[15] This conviction was borne home to him because he saw a world that had "come of age."[16] It no longer found any need to fall back on God to solve its problems. In the future, he argued, we can no longer depend upon men turning to God in their need. We must find God in what we know, not what we do not know. We must find him in our strength and health, not in our weakness and despair.[17] We must find a nonreligious way of presenting the Christian faith, for man is outgrowing religion.[18]

Bonhoeffer did not have the opportunity of developing his thought, and just where he was moving is not clear. His terse comments have proved to be a pregnant source for theological thinking and have been developed by several writers in directions that are often mutually contradictory. Bonhoeffer recognized that the traditional language of the Church is a liability today. But if we read him more closely, we find that he recognized the paradox about this language that we have noted; it is also an asset.[19] Thus he confessed that the problem of trying to work out a "nonreligious" interpretation of Biblical terminology was a bigger job than he had anticipated.[20]

The contemporary preoccupation of theology with communication is illustrated by the popularity of Anglican Bishop John Robinson's controversial book *Honest to God*. It makes no pretense at originality, but it puts into popular language a number of concerns found in recent theology. Robinson's primary concern is that there is a growing gulf between the traditional categories in which the Christian faith has been represented and the categories in which modern man does his thinking.[21] He goes so far as to suggest that we might have to discard the word "God" if the Gospel is to have significance. In particular, he believes that the picture of God "up there" is incomprehensible to modern man. The time has come to replace the concept of a "supernatural" God with that of God as the Ground of Being. We must no longer think of God in the heights: we must see him as the depth of life. It must be confessed that the reader puts down this book without a clear picture of what Robinson is proposing. The Archbishop of Canterbury was quoted in the public press as saying that he did not believe Robinson was heretical but was "only confused." Not many readers would deny that Robinson is both confused and confusing, but he cannot be discarded for that reason. The questions he has raised have expressed the problems that many find in the language of the Christian faith today. His confusion itself makes him a spokesman for many.

The defenders of traditional Christian language have not been silent. As responsible a thinker as Nels Ferré can go so far as to charge Tillich and Bultmann with presenting a "neo-naturalism."[22] He charges that these two men, in somewhat different ways, have eliminated any traditional form of God's transcendence, the reality of God's person, the hope for life after death, and the Incarnation. This brings Ferré to the conclusion that the issue presented by these men means nothing less than whether or not we should go "post-Christian."[23]

In light of such developments it is becoming evident that the old theological labels of "fundamentalist," "conservative," "liberal," "neoliberal," and "neoorthodox" are no longer adequate to represent the living issues in theology. In fact, they are positively misleading. If neoorthodoxy represented a "postliberal" movement, we today are witnessing a "post-neoorthodox" movement. We cannot foretell the shape of the new era in theology, but one thing is clear: the question of Christian language will remain central to theology.

When we see the concern of modern theology with problems of communication and language, we recall that language has been for some time the primary concern of the prevailing philosophy in Anglo-Saxon countries. Theology has been slow to take seriously the currents of analytical philosophy. Strangely enough, most theologians who have wrestled with the problems of language have looked to existentialist philosophy and have ignored the analysts. But in view of the language problems faced by theology today, it would seem that the time has come to ask whether philosophical language analysis may not have something to teach the theologian about the nature and use of language. In the rest of this book we shall attempt to enter into a conversation with this philosophy to see if such a conversation can illuminate the theological discussion of language.

It is important that we clarify what we mean in this study by "theological language" and "theology." First, we are limiting these terms to Christian theology. This is not because we suppose that only Christians have theology but because it would be presumptuous for the Christian to attempt to speak for the theology of any other religion. Secondly, except where it is made clear that we are doing otherwise, the term "theologian" will be applied to any Christian who speaks about God and not just to the minority within the Church who are known professionally as "theologians." The professional theologian has, we believe, a particular task in the community of faith, but we would argue that he has to work with the same language and has the same problems as the church-school teacher, the preacher, and the layman who wishes to say something about God. Of course, we shall draw much on the insights of professional theologians, but the language and the problems we have in mind are in no sense a monopoly of this professional group.

It is also important to define what we mean by a "conversation." A conversation implies two distinct parties on speaking terms with each other. Unfortunately theology often has not been on speaking terms with analytical philosophy. A conversation implies a willingness on both sides to listen as well as to speak. It does not imply that one party will dominate or absorb the other party, nor does it imply that we are simply seeking to score points by proving the other party to be in the wrong. It does imply that there is hope for mutual understanding.

There are a number of reasons why such a conversation is important and overdue. In the first place, theology must be in continual conversation with the cultural forms of the world in which it finds itself. Today a most important segment of our intellectual culture is analytical philosophy. Frederick Ferré tells us that wherever he has gone he has found educated Christians in Britain and America concerned and anxious about the relations, if any, between the methods of modern philosophy and the validity of theological affirmations.[24] Since the influence of this philosophy is spreading far beyond the confines of philosophy departments, it would be most unfortunate if theology did not pay attention to it.

In the second place, it is obvious, as Ferré indicates, that the new philosophy is seen by many as a threat to all theological language. Other ages have faced the claim that theological language is untrue. But today we face the claim that language about God is neither true nor false: it is without meaning. Such a claim cannot be ignored by the Church.

In the third place, we enter this conversation asking what theology can learn from this philosophy. Since the Christian faith is by nature a communicating and speaking faith, it needs to understand the nature of the language it uses. Unless we suppose that theological language is qualitatively different from all other language, it seems likely that a philosophy which deals with language would have some help for theology. Even if we should find that it has no help to offer theology, that in itself would be a most illuminating conclusion, and the reasons for it should be examined carefully.

Finally, we enter this conversation to see what theology may be able to contribute to the philosophical discussion. As we shall see, the contemporary analytical philosophers claim that it is their job to analyze language as it is actually used. It can hardly be denied that an important part of living language is language about God. When analytical philosophers analyze scientific language, they converse with the scientists to keep the philosophical analysis correlated with what is actually being done in the sciences. Unfortunately, analytical philosophers have not always shown the same desire to speak with either professional theologians or Christian laymen about theological language. But it seems reasonable that the Christian can enter the conversation with the real expectancy that he too will have something to contribute.

In light of these reasons for entering into conversation with analytical philosophy we shall in the next three chapters try to listen to it. In the remaining chapters we shall try to speak for theology in the light of what we have heard. We do not expect that our conversation will solve all problems or result in some kind of finality. We do hope that it will illuminate theological communication and that it will stir others to carry on this conversation.

NOTES

[1] See August B. Hollingshead and Fredrick C. Redlich, *Social Class and Mental Illness* (John Wiley & Sons, Inc., 1958), chap. 11.

[2] See C. W. Kegley and R. W. Bretall (eds.), *The Theology of Paul Tillich* (New York: The Macmillan Company, 1952), p. 334.

[3] Paul Tillich, *Systematic Theology,* Vol. I (Chicago: University of Chicago Press, 1951), p. 238.

[4] Walter Kaufmann, *Critique of Religion and Philosophy* (New York: Harper & Brothers, 1958), p. 140.

[5] Paul Tillich, *Systematic Theology,* Vol. II (Chicago: University of Chicago Press, 1957), p. 9.

[6] Paul Tillich, *Dynamics of Faith* (New York: Harper & Brothers, 1957), p. 41.

[7] *Ibid.,* p. 43.

[8] *Ibid.,* pp. 46–47.

[9] Paul Tillich, *Systematic Theology,* Vol. I, p. 240.

[10] George Tavard, *Paul Tillich and the Christian Message* (New York: Charles Scribner's Sons, 1962), p. 59.

[11] Tillich, *Dynamics of Faith,* p. 47.

[12] See F. E. Johnson (ed.), *Patterns of Faith* (New York: Harper & Brothers, 1957), p. 157.

[13] H. W. Bartsch (ed.), *Kerygma and Myth,* transl. by R. H. Fuller (London: S.P.C.K., 1954), pp. 3–8.

[14] *Ibid.,* pp. 10–11.

[15] Dietrich Bonhoeffer, *Prisoner for God,* ed. E. Bethge, transl. by R. H. Fuller (New York: Macmillan Company, 1960), pp. 140–141.

[16] *Ibid.,* p. 146.

[17] *Ibid.,* pp. 142–143.

[18] *Ibid.,* p. 122.

[19] *Ibid.* See pp. 140–141, 129–130, 164, 168–169.

[20] *Ibid.,* p. 162.

[21] J. A. T. Robinson, *Honest to God* (Philadelphia: Westminster Press, 1963), p. 8.

[22] Nels Ferré, *Searchlights on Contemporary Theology* (New York: Harper & Brothers, 1961), chaps. 10, 11.

[23] See Nels Ferré, book review of "*The Spirit of Protestantism,*" *Union Seminary Quarterly Review,* XVII, No. 1 (November, 1961), 104.

[24] Frederick Ferré, *Language, Logic and God* (New York: Harper & Brothers, 1961), p. vii.

2

THE BIRTH OF ANALYTICAL PHILOSOPHY

Twentieth century theology has engaged in many debates over the question of the proper relationship between philosophy and theology. On the one hand were philosophical theologians who agreed that theology must build on the insights of philosophy, although they could not agree as to which philosophy should provide the insights or how theology should incorporate them. Opposite these men have been arrayed those, sometimes called "kerygmatic" theologians, who insisted that revelation, not philosophy, is the only source for theology. In between were various views that preserved the independence of theology from philosophy while leaving it open to contributions from philosophy.

A major irony of these theological debates is that, with minor exceptions, they have been carried on with scant reference to what is happening in philosophy. More ironical still, it is often the philosophical theologian who is the furthest from the contemporary philosopher. An illustration of this irony is found in a story told by J. H. Randall. Paul Tillich, dean of philosophical theologians, was reading a paper to a group of philosophers among whom was G. E. Moore, a dean of contemporary philosophy. When Tillich finished his paper, Moore arose to say: "Now really, Mr. Tillich, I don't think I have been able to understand a single sentence of your paper. Won't you please try to state one sentence, or even one word, that I can understand?"[1] This failure of a leading philosophical theologian to communicate with a leading philosopher is symbolic of the gap that has widened between theology and philosophy. Before we write off this anecdote as merely an idiosyncrasy of Moore, we note that a philosopher of religion, J. H. Thomas, charges that despite Tillich's concern with philosophy he has ignored contemporary philosophy in the English-speaking world.[2]

The gap between theology and philosophy is due partly to the revolution that has occurred in philosophy in the last forty years.[3] The nature of this revolution is not easy to describe, for within its ranks are diverse viewpoints. Led by men like G. E. Moore, Bertrand Russell, and Ludwig Wittgenstein, it has won followers as diverse as Rudolf Carnap, A. J. Ayer, Richard Von Mises, Herbert Feigl, John Wisdom, Gilbert Ryle, R. M. Hare, John Hospers, Anthony Flew, Stuart Hampshire, and a host of others. It is unfortunate that even today many people refer to the whole movement as "logical positivism." This designation overlooks the fact that logical positivism was never more than one aspect of the movement and a somewhat "Peck's Bad Boy" aspect at that. The total movement is more correctly referred to as "analytical philosophy," "linguistic analysis," "linguistic philosophy," or "language philosophy." Most of its exponents object to party labels and prefer to speak of themselves simply as philosophers or, more technically, to say that they are "doing philosophy." We shall, for convenience, use the term "analytical philosophy" to refer to the movement as a whole, but this usage should not obscure the many differing positions that are covered by the term.

Although the defenders of analytical philosophy delight in calling their movement a "revolution," it is nonetheless the heir of a number of past philosophical developments. There are many parallels between it and later medieval philosophers such as William of Occam. It inherits much from Immanuel Kant but looks with the greatest affection upon the British empirical tradition led by David Hume. It has been deeply affected by the rise of modern science and, in its logical positivist wing, tends to restrict philosophy to the philosophy of science.

To understand the rise of analytical philosophy we need to realize the crisis that philosophy has faced in the twentieth century. This crisis has forced philosophy to ask itself what is the reason for its existence. Is there any task left for philosophy to do that science cannot do better? Was Ezra Pound perhaps right when he said, "After Leibniz's time a philosopher was just a guy who was too damn lazy to work in a laboratory."?[4]

H. A. Hodges reminds us that philosophy, unlike toolmaking or artistic expression, does not seem to be coeval with man himself. What we know as philosophy began primarily in the millennium preceding Christ in the great Western cultural centers.[5] Philosophy, meaning love of wisdom, was that pursuit in which man sought to see his life as a whole and to bind his various concerns into a synthesis. All knowledge was grist for the philosopher's mill as he sought to answer the ultimate questions of man's destiny, nature, and reason to be. In philosophy man sought, by a rational effort, to discover the good, the true, and the beautiful.

Philosophy developed rapidly in the cultural centers of the West. Few pursuits of man have moved so quickly to fruition and maturity. For centuries, as Hodges puts it, "there was little else in philosophy but the attempt to dot the 'i's and cross the 't's of Plato and Aristotle."[6] It was not until the eighteenth and nineteenth centuries that the question was raised seriously as to whether there was any legitimate place for the philosophical disciplines. By then it had become plausible to suppose that philosophy was a pursuit which arose within a particular community at a particular stage of cultural development and which would disappear with the passing of that stage. Auguste Comte was not the first nor the last to suggest that philosophy has had its day and is destined for extinction by the growth of science.

In the twentieth century the crisis for philosophy became acute. In former centuries the philosopher was a man of prestige who could speak with authority in areas of astronomy, physics, biology, and any other sphere of knowledge, and expect to be listened to with respect. But by the twentieth century the philosopher had learned from many burned fingers that philosophy could not pontificate on scientific matters. One time-honored philosophical question after another had been turned over to the appropriate science. As Gilbert Ryle puts it, "Sterile of demonstrable theorems, sterile of experimentally testable hypotheses, philosophy was to face the charge of being sterile."[7]

The reaction to the crisis has been varied. In Europe philosophers began to develop existentialism, which broke from former methods of philosophy. In man's inner life of anguish, decision, and self-examination, existentialists tried to find a realm that was untouchable by science and worthy of philosophical efforts. Roman Catholics dug in behind ancient barricades and called for a neo-Thomism in which "being" was the subject matter that was beyond science and hence open for philosophy. In Scandanavian and Anglo-Saxon countries it became increasingly evident that the various forms of analytical philosophy were to be philosophy's answer to the claim that it was obsolete. Even a cursory reading of philosophical journals or a glance at philosophical faculties in Great Britain or America will make it clear why Morton White named his book on twentieth century philosophy *The Age of Analysis.*[8]

Faced with the question of what task is left for philosophy, the analytical philosophers answered that the real task of philosophy is still open. It is what philosophers have been doing even when they may have thought they were doing something else. Philosophy's task is to study the nature of man's language and communication through language. To do this it is necessary to analyze logical forms, the nature of evidence, the meaning and purpose of propositions, and the general rules of discourse. As one philosopher quaintly put it, the purpose of philosophy is to see "how words behave." The great questions of the analytical philosopher came to be "What *do* you mean?" "What kind of statement is that?"

The purpose of the new philosophy was summed up by Wittgenstein when he said: "Philosophy is not a theory but an activity. . . . The result of philosophy is not a number of 'philosophical propositions,' but to make propositions clear."[9]

In the same vein J. O. Urmson can say, "There would be no need for philosophy if language were not inadequate."[10]

If philosophy is the analysis of language, many of the traditional concepts of philosophy disappear. Analytical philosophy makes no claim to judge the truth or falsity of factual statements, for it has no tools nor laboratory to test such statements. The task of philosophy with a statement is to ask what kind of statement it is, how it is used, what it means, how it would be verified or falsified, and then philosophy leaves any proof or disproof of the statement to the proper science or form of study.

Furthermore, philosophy abandons the whole field of metaphysics. It confesses that it has no tools with which it can investigate some realm beyond science or look at the world as a whole. Philosophy has no way of explaining the world; at best it can only analyze the language with which men do explain the world. However, as we shall see later, the analytical philosopher goes further than simply denying himself metaphysical probings; he finds that most metaphysics has arisen through misunderstanding the nature of language.

Analytical philosophy does not make value judgments. Philosophy cannot decide whether euthanasia is ethically justifiable, or whether we ought to underwrite birth-control programs in other countries. This does not mean that philosophers may not have strong views on these matters. They usually have. But their point is that they make their ethical decisions as responsible citizens, concerned human beings, and even perhaps as believing Christians. But as philosophers they can only ask: "What kind of statements are ethical statements?" "How are ethical statements used?"

The obvious reaction of one trained in classical philosophy is that analytical philosophers are irresponsible and trivial. They are avoiding the important and significant questions. They are continually sharpening the tools of thought, but they never get around to thinking with them. But analytical philosophers are not too perturbed by such charges. They will admit that this is their task—tool sharpening for thinkers. But, they go on, is that such a trivial task? Man is the communicating, hence speaking, animal. He must use language if he is to think or act. If the tools of language are dull, bent out of shape, or being used on material which they were never meant to cut, then all man's activities will suffer. Surely it is a most important task for someone to analyze the language that everyone uses so glibly and thoughtlessly. Thus, following Wittgenstein, the analytical philosopher thinks of his activity as a "therapy" for language.

In a very real sense analytical philosophy is philosophy become humble. The fact that many analytical philosophers fail to show humility does not change this fact any more than a lack of humility in many Christians disproves that Christianity is a religion that preaches humility. This is a remarkable development, for from the days of Plato there had been the assumption that the philosopher represented a superior type of person. (At least most philosophers believed this, and a large proportion of the laity was taken in.) Because he was trained in the ways of reason, the philosopher had knowledge where others had only beliefs. He had a superior ability to make moral judgments; hence Plato was certain that no state could be ideal until it had a philosopher for its king. A philosopher's sense of beauty was superior to that of hoi polloi. Few readers of Plato's dialogues can have failed to be annoyed at Plato's calm assumption that he is superior because he is of that rare species—a philosopher. This attitude was continued by later philosophers who had less justification than Plato for assuming it. In such a spirit philosophy has tended to promise salvation and a solution to all problems if only men would stop and listen to it.

The assumed superiority of the philosopher was seriously questioned by David Hume. Hume showed that there is no good reason for believing in the continuance of the physical universe when we are not observing it, the continuing existence of the human self, the operation of causality, the lawful operation of nature that is assumed in induction, and so on. He had no intention of casting out these beliefs, but he was concerned to demonstrate that all men accept them with what he called "natural belief." That is, the philosopher has no better reason for believing these vital presuppositions than the man on the street.

The analytical philosopher who denies that he can, as a philosopher, make superior ethical judgments or give a higher view of reality is, like Hume, denying that his philosophical status gives him an exalted height from which he can speak to the average man. Analytical philosophers would agree with Michael Frayn, writing in *The Guardian,* when he asks: Why should we expect philosophers to tell us how to arrange our lives? Why should they be any better at it than anyone else? This is what we mean by the humility of analytical philosophy.

During the twentieth century analytical philosophy has passed through several stages. Critics have tended to be gleeful about this, hailing the abandonment of each stage as a major defeat. But, in fact, one of the proofs of the dynamism of the movement is that it has been able to correct its own mistakes. The movement has had its periods of fanaticism and dogmatism, but what philosophical movement has not had this in its beginnings? What is remarkable is the speed and thoroughness with which the early positions have been revised. We shall not attempt to summarize fully the history of analytical philosophy, but we shall take note of some of its developments that are significant for the conversation between it and theology.[11]

G. E. Moore was a founder of analytical philosophy. Moore summed up his position as "A Defence of Common Sense."[12] Moore had no grand plan for explaining the universe; he simply sought to defend the common sense of man against the complexities created by philosophical sophistication. He did not claim that common sense is infallible, but he did believe that it could not be corrected until it was understood. Most philosophical confusions arise, he believed, because of fuzzy concepts of the questions involved or, perhaps, because several questions are treated as though they were one simple question. Only a patient analysis of the meaning involved can save the philosopher from useless efforts.

Contemporary with Moore were Bertrand Russell and his brilliant pupil Ludwig Wittgenstein. They produced a philosophy known as "logical atomism." This was based on the theory that all language can be analyzed into parts each of which mirrors a fact in the world. Thus, as reality is composed of atomic events, language is composed of corresponding atomic meanings.

Logical atomism analyzed two different forms of speech, a priori and empirical. A priori statements are those which are true by necessity; they cannot be false. They do not tell us about empirical existence, and they are neither confirmable nor falsifiable by empirical investigation. They are true because of the way in which we use words or symbols. A priori truths include all pure logic and mathematics. Logical truths are necessarily true because they are tautologies. The predicates of such sentences only make explicit what was already contained in the subject. To say that "all fathers have children" is an example of such tautologies. Mathematical truths are necessarily true because they simply express equality or identity.

This interpretation of a priori truths, made possible by modern mathematical discoveries, was a great advance for empiricist philosophy. A priori truths had always disturbed the empiricist because they seem to be known quite apart from any empirical evidence. Some hardy empiricists had said the reason we know that $2 + 2 = 4$ is that, as a matter of empirical experience, we had on many occasions taken two objects and two more and then we always found that we had four. But this reason is obviously false. $2 + 2 = 4$ cannot be false. If we had counted five after taking two groups of two, we would not change our mathematics, we would look for a magician, expect that we had made a mistake, or otherwise account for the anomaly. And so it would seem that mathematics is necessary and eternal truths, known in a quite unempirical manner. From the time of Plato such truths became a happy hunting ground for philosophers who wished to prove the existence of a non-space-time world. Furthermore, because a priori truths could not be wrong, they seemed to be the ideal example of truth. Empirical knowledge, which can often be wrong, suffered by comparison. The really real, it was argued, must belong to the realm of the eternally true and unchanging.

Mathematical and logical truths often have been used to prove the existence of God. Many truths of logic and mathematics, the argument goes, were undiscovered for thousands of years. Yet when these propositions were discovered it was obvious that they had not just begun to be true; they always had been true. The proposition that the square on the hypotenuse of a right triangle is equal to the sum of the squares on the other sides did not become true when or because Pythagoras formulated it. It was already true when he discovered it. Furthermore, such statements resist any effort at alteration. How can we understand the existence of such truths before and apart from the minds of men? Is it not necessary to postulate a superhuman mind or minds in which they have existed and continue to exist?

All such arguments are eliminated when we analyze the nature of such truths. $2 + 2$ has to equal 4 for the simple reason that $2 + 2$ is simply another way of saying 4. (This point may be clearer if, instead of writing $2 + 2 = 4$ we write ii + ii = iiii. The truth is necessary once we accept the principle of self-identity—a thing is what it is. Some years ago Popeye made famous the statement, "I yam what I yam." If we grant Popeye his point, all mathematics follows.

If mathematics and logic are necessarily true, they gain this necessity at the price of saying nothing about any reality beyond themselves. Although $2 + 2$ must always equal 4, this equation does not tell us about the physical world. For example, when we mix two quarts of water with two quarts of alcohol we do not end up with four quarts.

Mathematics and logic begin with certain rather arbitrary but useful definitions. Hence the axioms of Euclidean geometry start by defining straight lines and points in such a way that they could not exist in space. From these premises certain deductions can be made. All possible deductions are not immediately apparent, and this is why considerable time may pass before a Pythagoras "discovers" some of these deductions. If we had minds like an electrical computer, we would find little interest in mathematics or logic, for we would see instantly all the implications.

The arbitrariness involved in the selection of the axioms of a mathematical system became apparent when Lobachevski and others started with new axioms in which, for example, a straight line is not defined as the shortest distance between two points. From these axioms a new set of theorems follows and the square on the hypotenuse of a right triangle no longer equals the squares on the other two sides. Now which of these geometries is true? Which, we might ask, has been thought eternally by God? The only possible answer is "All and none." All are necessarily true in terms of the definitions from which they begin. None are true except on the basis of their own axioms. Which tells us about the "real world"? None of them. They are simply useful in varying degrees as we examine and measure the world. If we want to measure our gardens we shall find the Euclidean geometry most useful, but if we want to do a problem in atomic physics or astronomy, the chances are that we shall choose one of the non-Euclidean geometries. It will be understood why Russell could comment sarcastically: "Thus mathematical knowledge ceases to be mysterious. It is all of the same nature as the 'great truth' that there are three feet in a yard."[13]

This analysis of the nature of mathematics and logic was devastating to much of classical metaphysics. Such metaphysics had begun with certain "self-evident" truths and from these had deduced what must be true of existence. But it now became apparent that such argument is illogical in principle, for logic cannot tell us what must be true of existence. We can get nothing out of a logical argument that we did not put into it at the beginning.

The second type of speech that logical atomism described was empirical language. Whereas a priori speech is necessarily true, empirical statements cannot be necessarily true. Their truth or falsity can be decided only by examining the empirical world. If I say that "the chair occupies space," the statement is true by definition and there is no need to look at the chair to verify it. A "chair" that did not occupy space would not be a chair. But the statement tells nothing about any particular chair or even whether chairs exist. It is equally true that "the unicorn has a horn in his head." But if I say that "the chair is red," we must look at the chair to see if the statement is correct. All empirical statements can be wrong; they are never necessarily true. But if they lack the necessary nature of a priori statements, they can do what a priori statements cannot do: they can tell us about that which exists. It is thus made clear that a priori and empirical statements differ in their logical analysis, in their method of verification, and in the way in which they are used. Only error can result if we overlook these differences.

Logical atomism had a short life. Wittgenstein himself, in his later writings, demolished the position. It would not serve our purpose to trace the full story of its downfall, but we might note that it was primarily the metaphysical aspects of the system that caused it to be discarded. As J. O. Urmson says, it was not that the metaphysics of logical atomism was found wanting, it was rather that the analysts were growing suspicious of all metaphysics as such.[14]

Even before logical atomism fell, logical positivism was taking the center of the analytical stage. This movement was founded in Vienna by the so-called "Vienna Circle." Its members, including Morris Schlick, Rudolf Carnap, Victor Kraft, Herbert Feigl, and Otto Neurath, were primarily scientists rather than philosophers. In view of the fact that it is common to speak of all analytical philosophers as "logical positivists," it is well to recall that analytical philosophy had a good start before the Vienna Circle appeared.

It is appropriate to speak of logical positivism in the past tense, for today it is almost impossible to find an important thinker who would call himself a logical positivist or defend its program. Nonetheless, we must examine the position carefully. Although logical positivism is without major spokesmen, many camp followers are not yet prepared to abandon the ranks. Ayer's classic presentation of the position, *Language, Truth, and Logic,* is still a best seller in university book stores, and its simple, straightforward position is highly appealing to undergraduates. Furthermore, many philosophers who, because of weaknesses in the position, do not want to be responsible for defending logical positivism, are nonetheless quite ready to act as though it were valid when it serves their purpose.

Logical positivism attacked all forms of metaphysics and most of the traditional pursuits of philosophers. Believing that philosophy should deal only with logic and the sciences, it reduced philosophy to the philosophy of science. Taking the logical-atomist position on the nature of a priori and empirical statements, logical positivism limited all meaningful discourse to these two forms of language.

Central to logical positivism was the "verification principle." As A. J. Ayer defined it, "A sentence is factually significant to any given person if, and only if, he knows how to verify the proposition which it purports to express—that is, if he knows what observations would lead him, under certain conditions, to accept the proposition as being true, or reject it as being false."[15] In other words, a meaningful statement claims that a certain state of affairs exists that would not exist if the statement were false. Verification occurs if we look and find the state of affairs, and falsification occurs if we look and do not find the situation or if we find another situation that is incompatible with it. But if a statement is made and we have no idea where to look for verification or falsification, the statement has no meaning to us.

This does not mean that every meaningful statement must, in fact, be verifiable or falsifiable. The statement that "Julius Caesar had porridge for breakfast before he crossed the Rubicon" may be fruitless since, in fact, it cannot now be verified. But it is not meaningless or nonsensical in the logical-positivist sense because, in principle, we do know how such a statement could be verified or falsified. Similarly, although the statement that the other side of the moon is made of green cheese may seem nonsense in the common meaning of the word, it is not nonsense in the logical-positivist sense because we know what would verify it albeit at the present time we cannot get to the other side of the moon to do so. But if we do not know what could verify or falsify a statement, it cannot be meaningful to us.

The verification principle is further modified by pointing out that to be meaningful a statement does not need to be finally proved nor disproved. If we find evidence that tends to support or tends to negate a statement, then obviously it is meaningful even though a final proof is lacking. Since the logical positivist does not believe that empirical statements can be absolutely verified, the test of meaning often becomes "What would tend to falsify the statement?" If no evidence could count against the statement, it has asserted nothing.

At first sight this verification principle seems innocent enough. Surely if we mean something by a statement, we must have in mind some way in which, at least in principle, it can be verified or falsified. The principle begins to raise doubts when we see how logical positivism used it to limit the possibilities of meaningful discourse. It pointed out that empirical statements are verifiable by reference to sense data and that a priori statements are tested by reference to our dictionaries or the axioms of our mathematical system. A priori statements, although meaningful, cannot tell us about existence; they have no factual content. They tell us only how language is used. To have factual content, Ayer tells us, a statement must therefore be an empirical hypothesis.[16] It is obvious that, in fact, people make many statements that are neither true a priori nor are they empirical hypotheses. For example, they call things good and beautiful, and they refer to the will of God. But all such statements are shown by the verification principle to be "emotive." This means that they do not describe any reality, they express the attitudes or feelings of the speaker. Logical positivists also call such statements "nonsense" which in effect means that they are not based on any sensory experience, that is, they are non-sense.

One of the major uses of the verification principle in logical positivism was to reject all metaphysics. Ayer says, "We may accordingly define a metaphysical sentence as a sentence which purports to express a genuine proposition, but does, in fact, express neither a tautology nor an empirical hypothesis."[17] No metaphysician would want to admit that he had spoken only tautologies, for then he could not have said anything about the existing world; he would only be informing us about how he uses language. But if the metaphysician claims that he is making statements that are empirical hypotheses, then what he says must be open to study by science. And to make scientific statements without scientific investigation is an unenviable position. There seems nothing left for metaphysics but to be swallowed by science or to be cast into the category of the emotive, meaningless and nonsensical.

For logical positivism pure ethical statements are not statements of fact, and therefore they are not "significant" propositions. When I say, "It is wrong to do this," I am not making a statement about the act in question, I am expressing my attitude toward the action in question. Instead of saying, "It is wrong," I could equally well have said "Ugh!" Thus it is impossible to disagree about ethical statements. What does happen in cases of ethical disagreement is normally that we disagree about certain facts in the case. But if, having agreed on all the facts, our opponents still disagree with us, we write them off as having an inadequate moral nature. Reason cannot persuade them.

It is obvious what will happen to theological statements in this critique. We cannot verify statements about the existence of God through a priori methods, such as the ontological argument, for a priori arguments cannot tell about existence. This leaves theological statements only one path if they are to escape being relegated to the category of emotive and nonsense. They must pass the test as empirical hypotheses. But the difficulty is that the theologian wishes to speak of a God who is, in some sense, transcendent. Thus, if he wishes to use the teleological argument for God from the order of nature, he wants to establish more than that there is an order in nature. Of course, if we redefine God to equal the order that we find in nature, the teleological argument proves God's existence, but this is hardly a victory for theology. But if we believe that God is more than the order of nature, it is just this "more" that the order of nature cannot prove. It is no longer an empirical hypothesis. As Ayer puts it, if the existence of God were an empirical hypothesis, "it would be possible to deduce from it, and other empirical hypotheses, certain experiential propositions which were not deducible from those other hypotheses alone. But in fact this is not possible."[18] Thus statements about God are metaphysical and therefore meaningless and nonsensical.

Logical positivism gives the theologian two items of cold comfort. First, if the theist is speaking nonsense when he says that God exists, the atheist is speaking equal nonsense when he says that God does not exist. And, secondly, it is sometimes granted that the theologian, like the poet, may be speaking "important" nonsense.

We said earlier that logical positivism has lost its hold on the leading thinkers, if not on all of the camp followers. Thus Ayer, its foremost exponent in Great Britain, has conceded that it is now a past phenomenon.[19] There are many reasons for this. Some of them will be treated in the next chapter when we see how later analytical philosophy has developed. But here we shall point up just two flaws in logical positivism.

The first flaw is a strange one to find in a system dedicated to the careful analysis of language. Whereas the logical positivist carefully analyzed scientific and a priori statements, he had a strange blindness to the significance of other statements. Instead of analyzing them he tossed them into the wastebasket of "emotive language." This meant that ethical, aesthetic, and theological language were thrown indiscriminately into a heap that contained such other language forms as commands, ejaculations, statements about other minds, and nonsense verse. As we shall see in the next chapter, a major concern of recent analytical philosophy has been to analyze the meaning of these discarded types of language.

Instead of analyzing these many propositions the logical positivists described them in strangely emotional terms. Words with desirable connotations, such as "meaningful," "factual," "cognitive," and "sensible," were reserved for the language of science and logic. On the other hand, words that have pejorative connotations, such as "meaningless," "nonsensical," and "emotive," were applied to all other uses of language. When a man speaks with ethical conviction, or expresses appreciation of a beautiful picture, or puts forward a metaphysical theory upon which he has worked painstakingly, he is not likely to take kindly to someone who calls his speech "nonsense." "Nonsense" is a word of abuse normally used to insult the speaker. Surely logical positivists were not unaware of these emotional connotations of their language.

If the first flaw in logical positivism was a neglect of certain language forms and a description of them in emotional rather than analytical terms, the second flaw was more serious. It became evident that logical positivism's crusade against metaphysics was itself metaphysical. The metaphysical nature of logical positivism is revealed when we ask what kind of statement is its own verification principle. Logical positivism allows only two possibilities if it is to be meaningful. Its statement must be a priori or empirical. Some of the early logical positivists tried to argue that it is an empirical hypothesis, but it is clear that it is not. There is no empirical evidence that could tend to verify or falsify it. Therefore it is evident that, if the verification principle is not to fall into the emotive category, it must be a priori, a definition. In the Introduction to the second edition of *Language, Truth and Logic,* written ten years after the body of the book, Ayer concedes that the verification principle is meant to be a definition.[20] Thus it seems that all the metaphysician has to do is to say, "That is not how I define 'meaningful,'" and then he may go on to construct metaphysical systems without paying further attention to logical positivism.

The logical positivist was caught on the horns of his own dilemma. It is obvious that, in fact, the logical positivist believed that only a priori and empirical statements have meaning or significance. Because he believed this he believed that metaphysics was, by nature, nonsensical. But how was he to justify his position without committing metaphysical nonsense? Ayer is a typical logical positivist when he says that it is the mistake of metaphysicians that they make presuppositions that are not empirically verifiable and then deduce systems from them.[21] But now it is obvious that logical positivism has done exactly this. Its verification principle is not empirically verifiable, yet from it is deduced the whole logical positivist system.

Faced with this dilemma, Ayer tries to argue that, although the verification principle is a definition, it is not an arbitrary one. He grants that other definitions of meaning may be used, but, he argues, other definitions of meaning "would not be capable of being understood in the sense in which either scientific hypotheses or common-sense statements are habitually understood."[22] This interesting statement is worthy of comment. First, let us take the reference to "common sense." A reference to common sense is always ambiguous. Whose sense is common? Is A. J. Ayer's sense the common sense or not? Perhaps this is meant to be an appeal to common usage, but if so, it is simply false. The average person does not use "meaning" in such a way that it cannot be applied to ethical, aesthetic, or theological statements. It would seem that Ayer's appeal to common sense is an appeal to what he believes *ought* to be common sense. But that makes the statement, by Ayer's own definitions, an emotive statement.

Ayer's reference to science, however, seems to be on more solid ground. The verification principle is a useful description of meaning as it applies to science. As such it is a contribution to thought. If we are to understand what the logical positivist is really saying, we need to translate his words. Wherever we find him speaking of meaningful propositions we should translate "meaningful" to read "verifiable by science or logic." Where he says "emotive" or "meaningless" we simply translate "without scientific or definitional verification." When we so translate the logical-positivist claims they make considerable sense. Ethics, aesthetics, and theology are clearly not verifiable either scientifically or by definition. This might not seem too important until we recall how many books have been written in the past century to interpret theology as an empirical science or to propose a "scientific ethic." Against such claims logical positivism has made an important point.

This brief survey of its history reveals that soon after analytical philosophy appeared two of its major schools of thought were abandoned. But in renouncing these positions analytical philosophy moved into stronger positions, not into obscurity. Furthermore, positive gains had been made by these two movements before they passed from the scene.

It is evident that the ideal of forming a perfect language which haunted both logical atomism and logical positivism has gone the way of other utopian dreams. Logical atomism's metaphysics has proved unconvincing, and logical positivism's pretense to end all metaphysics produced another metaphysics. But, as J. O. Urmson puts it, " 'Classical' logical positivism may be dead, but it did not live in vain."[23]

Logical atomists and logical positivists made a real contribution to thought when they analyzed the difference between various types of statements. Their clear-cut distinction between empirical and a priori statements is a major step forward in philosophy. Ever since the early Greeks, philosophers have been intoxicated with the "eternal" necessity of mathematical and logical statements. When empirical and other statements could not produce such eternal certainty, they were discredited by comparison. Now we can see the nature of the eternal truths of mathematics and logic. They remain eternal truths only so long as they do not attempt to tell about anything beyond themselves. To try to pattern all thinking after the ideal of logic and mathematics is vain and useless. Other kinds of statements are not meant to do what these statements do. Furthermore, this analysis helps us to see that it is impossible to move from one type of statement to another. A priori truths can lead to no conclusions about physical existence, and empirical evidence can result in no necessary conclusions.

The early analysts have passed from the scene, but before they passed they added new zest and life to the philosophical discussion. They cast new light on some old issues, but, most important, they brought some clarification of the kinds of language statements we make. We shall see in the next chapter how this clarification has been developed.

NOTES

[1] C. W. Kegley and R. W. Bretall, *The Theology of Paul Tillich,* p. 133.

[2] J. H. Thomas, *Paul Tillich: An Appraisal* (Philadelphia: Westminster Press, 1963), p. 180.

[3] See A. J. Ayer et al., *The Revolution in Philosophy* (London: Macmillan, 1957).

[4] Quoted by A. G. N. Flew in A.G.N. Flew, *Logic and Language,* 2d series (Oxford: Basil Blackwell, 1955), p. 5.

[5] See F. W. Camfield (ed.), *Reformation Old and New* (London and Redhill: Lutterworth Press, 1947), pp. 184 ff.

[6] *Ibid.,* p. 185.

[7] Ayer, *et al., The Revolution in Philosophy,* p. 5.

[8] See Morton White, *The Age of Analysis* (New York: Mentor Books, 1955).

[9] Ludwig Wittgenstein, *Tractatus Logico-Philosophicus* (London: Routledge & Kegan Paul, 1955), p. 77.

[10] J. O. Urmson, *Philosophical Analysis* (Oxford: Clarendon Press, 1956), p. 50.

[11] For a more extensive history of the movement see J. O. Urmson, *op. cit.*

[12] See J. H. Muirhead (ed.), *Contemporary British Philosophy* (New York: Macmillan Company, 1953), pp. 191–223 (second series).

[13] Morton White, *op. cit.,* p. 198.

[14] J. O. Urmson, *op. cit.,* p. 99.

[15] A. J. Ayer, *Language, Truth and Logic* (New York: Dover Publications, 1946), p. 35.

[16] *Ibid.,* p. 41.

[17] *Loc. cit.*

[18] *Ibid.,* p. 115.

[19] Ayer, *et al., The Revolution in Philosophy,* p. 73.

[20] Ayer, *Language, Truth and Logic,* p. 16.

[21] *Ibid.,* pp. 46–47.

[22] *Ibid.,* p. 16.

[23] J. O. Urmson, *op. cit.,* p. 129.

3

THE MATURING OF ANALYTICAL PHILOSOPHY

G. H. Von Wright tells us that Wittgenstein inspired two important schools of thought, which he identifies as "logical positivism" or "logical empiricism" and the "so-called analytic or linguistic movement."[1] Von Wright would agree with a growing number of philosophers who object to the use of the term "analytical philosophy" to describe both of these movements. To include both under the same term hides the fact that the later work of Wittgenstein brought about a major philosophical revolution. "The author of the *Philosophical Investigations* has no ancestors in philosophy," argues Von Wright.[2] There is much to justify this claim, although one might ask whether the early Wittgenstein was not at least an "ancestor" of the later Wittgenstein in that the earlier work was a blind alley that had to be explored before the later work could progress.

We shall leave it to the philosophers to decide whether the later Wittgenstein created a new philosophy or brought about a "Protestant Reformation" in analytical philosophy. Until philosophers themselves are more in harmony, we can proceed for our purpose by using the term "analytical philosophy" to refer to the movement from Moore through the followers of the later Wittgenstein. To remind ourselves of the crucial changes inspired by Wittgenstein, however, we shall use the term "linguistic analysis" to describe the trends inspired by the later Wittgenstein. To give a complete description of this philosophy, we would need to point to many variations within it, such as the difference between the British and the American versions. But since our concern is to engage in a conversation with this philosophy to see what light it can throw on theological language, we can concentrate on those of its features that are relatively common among those who "do" philosophy in this fashion.

In speaking of the "later Wittgenstein" we are referring to the work that follows his *Tractatus Logico-Philosophicus.* This is found in his posthumously published *Philosophical Investigations* and in *The Blue and Brown Books* which were dictated to his students.

H. D. Aiken is no doubt correct in saying that few philosophers in our century are likely to have more enduring fame than Wittgenstein.[3] Wittgenstein was a strange figure, an eccentric and troubled genius. Born in Vienna in 1889, he was destined to become a Cambridge professor.[4] He had the marks of a saint, not the least of which was that he would have scorned the suggestion as absurd. As in the case of most saints, it was not easy to be his friend, but those who were his friends found in him a deep and abiding inspiration. He gave away the fortune he inherited and lived a life of rigorous simplicity. His class lectures were delivered without notes and were composed during delivery through a give-and-take with his students. This philosophical genius preferred reading detective magazines to perusing the learned philosophical journal *Mind.* It is significant that the concept of God as Creator was beyond his comprehension, but he found deep meaning in the idea of a judging and redeeming God. In some ways he reminds us of Kierkegaard, and it could well be that, like Kierkegaard, he was so far ahead of his time that his work will come into its own only in the future. Perhaps it is correct to say that his later work "has no ancestors," but it will surely have important descendants.

In his early work Wittgenstein was dedicated to the idea that all language ought to fit the pattern of picturing atomic facts. Every meaningful word either pictures a fact in reality or it is a connecting word belonging to the logic of language. But as he begins his *Philosophical Investigations* it is immediately apparent that Wittgenstein has become aware that language is richer and more diverse than either he or the logical positivists had realized. We describe what language is, he says, but then we realize that, although we have described certain uses of language, there are other legitimate uses of language that have been omitted. It is as though someone defined games in terms of moving objects on surfaces according to rules. We would have to point out that he was describing board games, but that there are many other types of games that are not so described.[5]

This illustration leads Wittgenstein to wrestle with the problem of how to define games so that we can include everything we call games under the definition. It becomes evident that there are many games, often having contradictory features. When we have defined games as a test of skill and ability between opposing players someone mentions solitaire. We say, "If they are all called games, they must have something that is common to all of them." But, Wittgenstein demands, what is the common meaning implied in war games, baseball, solitaire, and bouncing a ball? It is perhaps natural to suppose that there is some reality or essence that corresponds to every word we use. But is there? We find that every game has something in common with some other game, but we fail to discover features common to all activities called games. We find a "family resemblance." When we say that members of a family have a family resemblance we do not mean that any two members have identical features. Some have the same nose, others the same chin, and still others a similar way of walking. Similarly, each game has its own particular characteristics, its own rules. Although chess shares the family resemblance with checkers of being played on the same board, the rules of chess do not allow the taking of a piece by jumping over it as do the rules of checkers.

In a like manner, says Wittgenstein, we have a variety of language "games," each with its own particular characteristics and rules. Each game bears similarities to some other game, but there is no set of features to be found in all language games. It is no more legitimate to criticize a particular discourse because it does not follow the rules of some other discourse than it is to criticize the chess player for not obeying the rules of checkers. The logical positivist was right. The rules of discourse in ethics are not the same as the rules of empirical science, but that does not mean that ethical discussion is nonsense. Words are like the tools in a toolbox. Each tool has its own particular function, and it is silly to complain about the hammer because it will not cut wood. Similarly, there is no use deploring the fact that ethical words do not describe empirical realities; they are not meant to do so. Confusions in thought always occur when we suppose that all words must have the same kind of function and use.

Language has many uses, and it is continually growing as new knowledge and activities come into our experience. Wittgenstein was especially brilliant at imagining language systems quite different from ours and pointing out that to imagine a different language is to describe a different way of life.[6] We can imagine a language system that includes only commands. Do we say that this is an incomplete language? But when is our language complete? Men might have thought that their language was complete before the symbolism of chemistry and infinitesimal calculus came into it. But no limit can be put around the possible language games that we may come to play. Language arises in the environment of man's life and is used as a tool for the purposes of life. As our life increases in complexity we shall find language games to fit it.

The term "language game" is meant to point up the fact that the "*speaking* of language is part of an activity, or a form of life."[7] Therefore, to get at the meaning of a proposition, we need to find out what its use is. When we observe how words are actually used we find that there are far more jobs to do than most textbooks on logic would lead us to believe.

The failure to recognize different language games results in the attempt to force all language uses into a straitjacket of rules and regulations. We tend to think of all language as operating with the precision of calculus. This is like supposing that all games are neatly defined by rules as are baseball and chess. But two children may invent a game spontaneously as they play it.[8] Similarly, many important language uses are unstructured, and for Wittgenstein this is not a flaw but a virtue. They perform the function for which they are used because they do not have a more rigorous structure.

The recognition of varieties of language games leads Wittgenstein to recognize that there are many ways to verify statements, depending on the language game that is being played. From this it follows that there are various kinds of certainty.[9] Whereas logical positivism limited verification to empirical and logical propositions, Wittgenstein at least opens the door to the possibility of other forms of verification or validation. Man speaks meaningfully in terms other than logic and science, and he has certainties other than those of logic and science.

An interesting feature of Wittgenstein's thought is his theory that "philosophical problems arise when language *goes on holiday*."[10] That is, so long as we are using language, we know what we mean, we communicate. But when we are not actually using words but thinking about how we use them, we begin to see anomalies and puzzles. This reminds us of Augustine, who commented that he knew very well what time was until he was asked to explain it.

The primary task of philosophy, believes Wittgenstein, is to provide a therapy for language when it falls into confusing puzzles. Because problems arise when language is "on holiday" (or the engine of language is idling, to use another of Wittgenstein's analogies), it is necessary to take the puzzling proposition back to ordinary speech where it is used and understood. This technique has come to be known in linguistic analysis as the "appeal to the paradigm case."

Considerable criticism has been raised against the appeal to the paradigm case.[11] Critics have argued that it is a method which enables its users to evade the real problems and turn their attention to the obvious or the trivial. Instead of solving problems, appeal to a paradigm case discourages their being raised. These criticisms may be well taken against philosophers who have too easily supposed that an appeal to a paradigm case is a way out of all problems. But we need to go back and see how Wittgenstein really operates.

The major revolution of the later Wittgenstein came about when he called upon philosophers to ask not for the meaning of a word but for its use. It is a common supposition that words have certain meanings as an oak tree has oak leaves. This supposition was obvious in logical positivism's claims about the meaning of the word "meaning." But Wittgenstein came to see that, in fact, words are tools to be used for particular purposes. They have the meanings that men have given to them by using them. When we look for the meaning of words we should not operate as though words had meanings given to them by some independent power so that we could scientifically arrive at their *real* meaning. Rather, we have to analyze patiently how they are used in ordinary discourse.[12] We need to see how a word operates within the game of which it is a part.

When Wittgenstein so analyzed words he found that very frequently they do not have one precise meaning. Failure to see this results in a variety of puzzles and blunders. Thus the phrase "appeal to the paradigm case" does not describe Wittgenstein's analysis. Wittgenstein was never satisfied with *the* paradigm case of any word. As we follow him, we see that he tries to find several instances in which we would normally use the word but which bring out different shades of meaning. He asks how we would teach a child to use the word, how we would teach it to an adult who does not know our language. He imagines strange circumstances and asks whether we would still use the word. He compares it with various words that are similar to it but differ in significant ways. He tries to see where it would be obviously nonsensical to use it. As Wittgenstein pursues his analysis of what he calls the "grammar" of the word, its normal uses begin to appear. If any of his followers thought they could short-circuit the process by appealing to one paradigm case of a word, they could not look to Wittgenstein for support.

Far from dooming us to bypassing all problems by an appeal to a paradigm case, Wittgenstein finds that a very frequent source of logical confusion is the failure to see that words have a variety of uses with family resemblances rather than one set meaning. We become confused, for example, if we do not see that "proof" means something quite different in mathematics, physics, law courts, and personal relations. The word "language" itself has been a fruitful source of such confusions. We say that all activities called "language" *must* have something in common. But, Wittgenstein asks us to look and see—what is "common"? He reviews twenty different language uses, including giving orders, describing the appearance of an object, speculating about an event, making up a story, guessing riddles, making a joke, translating from one language to another, thanking, cursing, greeting and praying.[13] No such list could be complete, for new language uses are being found continually. Anyone who insists that there must be something common to all of these because they are all "language" will inevitably end up remaking certain language uses after the image of other uses, with the result that they will no longer be able to do what they were meant to do.

Wittgenstein does not deplore the variant shades of meaning that words have. It is a mistake of philosophy to suppose that it can or should improve upon ordinary language by creating ideal languages in which all words would have precise meaning.[14] Such a language would be poorer than ordinary language, for it would not be able to do the many tasks performed by ordinary language. The task of philosophy is not to create a new language but to help us escape from the blunders into which we fall when we misinterpret the "grammar" of ordinary language. Because of this the followers of Wittgenstein are often called "ordinary-language philosophers."

Wittgenstein was not unduly optimistic about what his technique could achieve. He notes that often we have to distinguish between "surface grammar" and "depth grammar." At first we are impressed by the way the word is used in a sentence, that is, with what we can take in by the ear. But then we note that it bears a depth of meaning that the surface grammar misses. From this he concludes, "No wonder we find it difficult to know our way about."[15] But if Wittgenstein does not promise to solve all problems, he is convinced that we cannot solve the complicated problems into which language leads us if we do not first understand language in contexts where the meaning is relatively simple and comprehensible.

It is often charged that, because of his appeal to common use of language, Wittgenstein does not provide any basis for criticizing or changing language use. Once we have found how a proposition is used, we cannot argue that the case is good or bad. We can show that a particular statement violates the rules of a language game, but we cannot ask if the rules "should" be violated. David Pole argues that "Wittengenstein's whole treatment of language takes no account of the necessity or possibility of its growth; one may go further, it comes near to prohibiting it."[16] This criticism is mistaken. From what we have said, it is obvious that Wittgenstein sees that language is in continual growth. But his point, which Pole seems to miss, is that such changes can occur only with changes in life itself. A philosopher sitting in his armchair may work out all kinds of changes in language practices and rules, but these remain his private language, of interest only to him, unless some change in life makes it a desirable and useful change in common language. Once again, we see the humility of philosophy in the analysts. The philosopher cannot be a creator of new language forms; he must serve the purpose of analyzing the language that our life has in fact produced. We might paraphrase Wittgenstein by saying that until the word has "become flesh" the philosopher cannot produce it from out of his thought.

Although Wittgenstein is most important as a clue to linguistic analysis, it must not be thought that linguistic analysis is simply Wittgenstein's "school." It is not a monolithic structure. It would be difficult to find a set of doctrines upon which its adherents agree. It is a movement sharing common methods and having some common ideas about how to "do" philosophy. Following Wittgenstein, it recognizes that language has many legitimate uses. Thus we do not find the linguistic analyst shouting, like the logical positivist, "You can't say that!"

One of the chief differences between linguistic analysis and logical positivism appears when we examine what happens to the category called "emotive" by logical positivism. Despite its pretension to be radically empirical and scientific, logical positivism was a strangely a priori system. It began by deciding a priori how language could be used and, by definition, divided language into three possible categories—empirical, a priori, and emotive. The emotive category was defined negatively as being anything that did not meet the requirements of the first two. As we noted in the last chapter, this kind of dogmatism sounds strange to the average person who knows that he is speaking meaningfully on many occasions when his words cannot be forced into the Procrustes' bed of empirical and logical statements. But linguistic analysis, following Wittgenstein, is much more truly empirical. It attempts to examine how, in fact, language is used.

As it examines language in actual use, linguistic analysis recognizes that there are many uses of words. Thus we must begin by asking what a sentence enables us to do. In many instances we find that a sentence is not meant to be an empirical description of the world. In such cases nothing is clarified by calling the sentence emotive or meaningless. Thus, whereas logical positivism placed all nonempirical and non-a priori statements into one category, emotive language, linguistic analysis has been patiently sorting out the various usages of language forms tossed into this basket.

When differing kinds of language usages are explored it is found that each has its own logic. Of course this is not to be taken literally to mean that every form of language has a logic totally different from every other one. As Wittgenstein saw, although he failed to find anything that all games had in common, every game had something in common with some other game. Similarly, there is an overlapping of language games. The use of a statement and its logic, however, are correlated, and one cannot verify a statement by using logical methods that are appropriate to a completely different kind of statement.

Whereas linguistic analysis sees that language has many uses, it also sees that it has many misuses, and it is convinced that a number of problems arise from such misuses. These are attempts to make a move in a language game that violates the rules of the game. It is like taking an opponent's piece in chess by jumping over it as one would do in checkers. The therapeutic function of philosophy is to reveal such misuses.

This means that philosophy must grapple with what Gilbert Ryle has called "systematically misleading expressions" and what John Wisdom calls "puzzles." That is, our language has ways of becoming misleading and puzzling. Where language presents us with such puzzles philosophy has to step in. As Wittgenstein put it, the purpose of philpsophy is to relieve "mental cramps."

Most linguistic analysts would see traditional philosophical debates about the existence of physical objects as arising from such puzzles. If I say that there is a cat on the chair, that is a normal, straightforward statement which everyone understands. And if someone denies it, that too is simple and straightforward. If we see and feel the cat and hear it meow, we take it for granted that the first statement is correct and the second false. There is no problem. On rare occasions we might still have an argument, but this would be treated under such concepts as hallucinations or tricks.

But in the history of thought many philosophers have been prepared to continue the argument after all normal arguments end. Some have said that we have the phenomenon of the cat but we cannot know what is really in the chair, the "thing-in-itself." Some have said that we have the thought of a cat in the mind of the Absolute which forms a percept in our minds. Some have argued that there is a cat just as we see and feel, for our minds grasp reality as it actually is. Some would argue that everything we see or feel is really an illusion. Some would argue that nothing exists but the thinker and the thoughts in his mind. The reader can fill in the various other ways in which philosophers have questioned the relation of the "appearance" to the "reality."

Now all of these statements, notes the linguistic analyst, are odd. They have no use in our normal way of talking. At first sight it may seem that such philosophers are trying to examine reality or, putting it more eloquently, they are discussing ontology. But none of these theories tells us anything about the cat. For all of these different philosophers the cat meows, gives birth to kittens, and sheds hair on the couch. The philosophers are not like the man who argues in ordinary conversation that the cat is not real. The latter has some alternative in mind; he is implying that I am having an illusion or that the cat is stuffed. We can settle the argument by examining the cat. But the philosophers have no such alternatives in mind. They agree that we shall see, feel, and hear the cat. Whether they argue for or against the "reality" of the cat, it is evident that by "real" they mean something different than what is meant in an ordinary discussion of cats.

The point is illustrated by a famous story about Samuel Johnson. When he heard of a philosophy that denied the reality of the material world Johnson said, "I refute it thus," kicking a rock. But of course he did not refute the philosophy, for the philosophers in question were sure that on kicking the rock Johnson would feel a pain in what he thought was his toe. What Johnson missed was that no actual happening could change the philosopher's theory, for the philosopher was not offering an alternative description of the rock to put into competition with the ordinary description of it. This is why Anthony Standen, tongue in cheek, suggested that in such cases you should kick not the rock but the philosopher.

It is obvious that these various philosophical theories, albeit they seem to be talking about cats or rocks, really have no interest in anything that enters into normal conversation. Are they talking about anything at all? The logical positivist would say, "No, this is nonsense pure and simple." The linguistic analyst is more charitable. These philosophers, he suggests, may have fallen into this puzzle by trying to recommend a use of language in a strange case. They are not describing some reality, not even a vague one like "being," but by changing our language uses they may bring to light something that might be overlooked. Thus, by making the odd statement that the cat does not "really" exist, or is just a "collection of percepts," and so on, they draw attention to the fact that knowledge comes solely through the senses and the mind.

Sometimes, as in the case of Hindu philosophy or Christian Science, the ploy is used to downgrade our evaluation of the importance of the material world. It is interesting that C. L. Stevenson has suggested that this is what logical positivism was trying to do when it called for a change in the normal use of the word "meaning."[17] By such a change it hoped to make people see the difference between science and metaphysics and consequently to downgrade the popular evaluation of metaphysics. Perhaps logical positivism was slow in seeing its own metaphysical nature because, traditionally, metaphysicians have called for a change in the use of words like "exist," "real," and "being," whereas the logical-positivist metaphysicians called for a change in the word "meaning."

The linguistic analyst sees a further use in such studies. Wrestling with these perplexities helps us see how language normally functions. Even though the philosophical discussion has not increased our knowledge of cats nor given us knowledge of "being," it has helped, by raising puzzles, to clarify the operation of language, and it brings out features of it that are often overlooked in normal discourse.

Of course the traditional metaphysician will not be overjoyed at this defense of his task. Certainly he has believed that he was doing something more than discussing language uses. He has believed that he was discussing reality on a level deeper than that of science or common sense. But at least his work has not been dismissed simply as nonsense.

Linguistic analysis finds a major source of puzzles in the fact that while two sentences may be grammatically parallel, their logic may be radically different. When this logical difference is overlooked there are various difficulties. We fail to see that the sentences belong to different language games and must be interpreted in different ways. Worse still, we may take expressions from one language game and put them into a sentence with words from another game in such a way that we get nonsense. To use one of Wittgenstein's examples, we tell time by reference to the position of the sun in relation to that point on the earth whose time we wish to tell. If someone asks, "What is the time on the sun?" he asks a question that has no use in the normal language game of telling time. It is like asking how many points a field goal counts in baseball.[18]

This aspect of language always has been exploited by humorists. When a word has two distinct meanings we get puns, and when a sentence puts two language games together we get a more subtle type of humor. Lewis Carroll was a master at this. We recall the King in *Through the Looking Glass* asking the messenger whether he passed anyone on the road. When the messenger replies that he passed "nobody," it starts a discussion. The king affirms that since the messenger passed "nobody," " 'nobody' walks slower than you." The messenger takes offense and argues, "I am sure that nobody walks much faster than I do." The king responds that if this were so, the messenger could not have passed "nobody." This bit of word play arises because the two sentences "I passed John" and "I passed nobody" are grammatically identical but logically quite different. The same aspect of language was exploited by the famous Abbott and Costello routine "Who's on first?"

All this seems trivial, and we may be tempted to complain that if philosophy cannot achieve something more profound, it ought to be relegated to musical comedy. However, is this so trivial? Thinkers like Heidegger and his disciples in theology have found important places in their systems for the concept of "nonbeing" or "nothingness." Have they been misled by the nature of language to suppose that they can talk about nothing as they can talk about birds and bees? Perhaps such thinkers are consciously using their terms in a strange fashion. But even so, as Mary Warnock notes, the using of the noun "nothingness" is almost bound to lead to trying to think of nothingness as a thing, albeit of a peculiar kind.[19]

Furthermore, many such mistakes due to grammar are not as clear as the humorous "nobody." From the time of Plato many philosophers have supposed that there must exist such entities as justice and virtue. Because grammatically the sentences "Candy is desirable" and "Justice is desirable" are similar, and because we can find candy existing, it is assumed that justice must likewise exist somewhere. Since justice is not located in the world of things as is candy, it becomes necessary to invent a world of ideas where justice has a form of existence vaguely analogous to candy's existence in this world. This misses the fact that justice belongs to a different language game than candy. Its logic is different.

The logical difference between justice and candy is so great that even the predicate "is desirable" takes on a different connotation. If a man says that to him candy is "not desirable," we are likely to reply with a shrug, "Every man to his taste." But if a man says that to him justice is "not desirable," we are almost certain to respond, "It ought to be!" Whereas Platonists have been misled by the grammar of the sentence to suppose that justice must exist as an entity somewhere, other philosophers have supposed that ethics are "purely a matter of taste."

Closely associated with this error is that which arises when grammar does not indicate that we have moved from premises to conclusions in a manner that violates the rules of meaningful language. This is to fail to see that two language games have been confused. Everyone has learned examples of such category confusions early in his education. It comes as a surprise to the youngster who has learned that two twos are always four to find that he cannot add two cats to two dogs and get four pigeons. He knows that "two plus two equals four" is a formula into which cats, dogs, or pigeons may be put without changing its truth. Why can they not all be put into it at the same time? Because to do so is to confuse categories.

This kind of logical confusion is a simple form of a mistake often made in complex forms. Thus when a man tries to deduce ethical statements from empirical facts he commits a dogs-plus-cats-equals-pigeons fallacy. Most ethical philosophers agree with G. E. Moore's criticism of the "naturalistic fallacy." That is, it is a fallacy to try to reduce ethical and moral terms to empirical statements. Furthermore, it is logically impossible to deduce ethical conclusions from factual premises. Of course, in any consideration of an ethical problem facts are relevant. If I am trying to decide whether it is my duty to feed a certain man, I need answers to such empirical questions as "Is the man in need of food?" and "Is he incapable of getting food for himself?" But from no list of empirical facts could it be deduced that I *ought* to feed him. If I am committed to the ethical premise that I ought to feed the needy, then empirical facts which show a man to be needy will lead to the conclusion that I ought to feed him. But without the ethical premise the facts would not lead to any ethical conclusion.

This is an important clarification. Because of the contemporary pre-eminence of the physical sciences it is a common argument that science must solve all our problems. And since it is obvious that our most pressing problems today are ethical, it is often claimed that we need a "scientific ethic."[20] If this means that in examining the facts, as we must do in all ethical decisions, we ought to use the findings of science, then it is obvious that we need a scientific ethic. But if, as is often the case, the defender of a scientific ethic believes that we can get our ethical ideals from science or scientifically verify our ethical ideals, then we have a notorious example of the naturalistic fallacy. Science can tell us that if we do *A* then *B* will result. But science cannot tell us whether we ought to seek *B*. If we accept the achievement of *B* as ethically desirable but find the doing of *A* ethically undesirable, science has no way of deciding whether *B* is worth the price of *A*. These are ethical decisions, and they have their own logic, their own game. The tools of science can no more jass judgment on them than they can pass judgment on the beauty of a symphony concert. The attempt to have scientists provide us with our ethical ideals is on a par with supposing that the persons best equipped to tell us how to shave are baseball stars.

It is important to see the meaning of "cannot" when we say that science cannot give us ethical ideals. It is not like saying that science cannot get us to the moon, for this is a provisional "cannot," and anyone who made the statement today would probably want to qualify it by adding "yet." We might hope to remove this "cannot." But in saying that science cannot give us ethical ideals we are saying that it logically cannot do so. It is like saying that we cannot have a square circle. It is a contradiction in terms.

Metaphysics is an area where linguistic analysts have found many categorical fallacies. The linguistic analyst has no quick method of banishing metaphysics as the logical positivist believed that he had. But the linguistic analyst has demonstrated that a goodly number of metaphysical arguments begin with empirical cats and end with metaphysical pigeons. All too often the metaphysician starts with words taken from common language games, but at some point he shifts into a completely different use of the word. This may be harmless, but if we do not know what is happening, we get into trouble. We kick rocks to disprove the claim that matter is "not real." The philosopher denying the reality of matter has taken the word "real" from the normal language games and has shifted to a new meaning. Whether this new meaning of "real" has some value in another language game is debatable, but if we do not see that we are no longer adding dogs and cats but playing with pigeons, we shall have nothing but confusion.

Another language confusion is to assume that an argument is about facts when it is really an argument about the use of language. For example, it is not difficult today to get into an argument over the question "Do computing machines think?" Yet it is clear that such arguments seldom persuade anyone. The question looks like "Do cats give birth to kittens?" But there is no normal argument about the latter question. We answer it by examining the behavior of cats. Why cannot we do the same for the thinking of computing machines? The debaters, if enlightened, will agree about what computing machines do—they solve mathematical problems, play chess, forecast election results, and so on. Where is their disagreement? It revolves around the meaning of "think." What seemed to be an empirical argument about computing machines turns out to be an argument about how we are to use the word "think." With computing machines a new activity has appeared that creates the problem as to the language game in which this activity should be located.

Here is a source of many annoying disagreements. Certain words take on strongly desirable or undesirable connotations but remain vague in meaning. The result is that arguments about them are inevitably frustrating. When a Communist argues that the people of communist countries are more free than those in a democracy, he is not simply pointing to facts: he is using a different meaning of "freedom" from that which is used in democratic societies. Likewise we can think of the decisionless battles that rage around words like "intelligence," "obscene," "equality," and "peace-loving."

In view of the problems that arise from within language itself, philosopher G. A. Paul can say of a typical philosophical problem, "The difficulty about it is not that there is a problem which we can understand and to which we are unable to find the answer; the difficulty is on the contrary to find out clearly what the problem is itself."[21] In many of the great philosophical debates through the ages we are beginning to see that a reason why no answer has been agreed upon is that no problem has been definitely identified. It may be that after a problem is identified the answer still will elude us. Analysis may show that there is no problem, that men have been misled by language to imagine a problem where none exists. And finally, of course, there is the hope that, having correctly identified a problem, we shall be able to obtain an answer.

Our purpose is to initiate a conversation between theology and analytical philosophy, not to make a critical evaluation of this philosophy. Such a task must be left to the philosophers. We might note, however, some critiques and evaluations that are made of analytical philosophy.

One critique can be dismissed quickly. This is the charge

that analytical philosophy is not philosophy. Compared with classical philosophers, the analysts have abandoned philosophical pursuits and are usurpers in philosophical departments. Since this is a problem arising from the definition of "philosophy," we can leave the debate to philosophers. If it should be agreed that this method is not philosophy, it would not disappear. It would still be with us as an intellectual influence no matter what we called it.

The second critique likewise may be dismissed. It is often claimed by other philosophers and by theologians that we can ignore analytical philosophy because it is only a "fad." The implication is that if we will ignore it, it will soon be as outdated as the Davy Crockett hat. It cannot be denied that analytical philosophy has taken on some of the marks of a fad. Furthermore, there are signs that the fad has passed the peak of its popularity. But this is hardly a serious criticism of its validity as an intellectual contribution. We must ask whether it has made any important contribution to thought. This cannot be answered if we refuse to enter into conversation with it.

A third critique, and perhaps what is really meant by the claim that it is not "philosophy," is that analytical philosophy has failed to deal with the "important" questions. It submerges itself in the problems of language and fails to tackle the great issues that face man. Such criticism usually points to the "great" issues treated by former philosophies such as the existence of God, the nature of being, the good, the true, and the beautiful. In contradistinction to this, notes the critic, the analyst is preoccupied solely with "language."

It is difficult not to have sympathy with this criticism, for analytical philosophers can become as arid and irrelevant as the mythical medievalists who debated about the number of angels that could dance on the head of a pin. Nonetheless, this cannot be taken as a final criticism. Analytical philosophy is young as philosophical schools count age. At first it was preoccupied with developing its new method. It is too early to say what it may be able to contribute to "important" questions. We need many conversations like the one in which we are engaged before we can weigh its contribution to various subjects. Even so, we would say that a number of important questions already have had considerable light cast upon them, and the analysts are beginning to turn to a wider range of problems.

The claim that analytic philosophy does not deal with "important" questions is often rooted in the tendency of popular thought to speak of "semantic problems" or "problems of language" as trivial. When we say that our differences are "only verbal" we feel that we have somehow resolved our problems. But actually this is a naïve view, and analytical philosophy has helped us to see its naïveté. No analytical philosopher would say that all problems are problems of language, but analytical philosophy has helped us to see that most problems involve problems of language. In view of the fact that man communicates and thinks with language, any "puzzles" or confusions in language are certain to create and magnify other problems. It may well be that other philosophers have wrestled with more "important" problems. But as one reads their efforts he often feels that they might have labored more fruitfully if they had begun with the analytic discipline. As J. L. Austin puts it, linguistic analysis, "if not the be all and end all, [is] at least the begin all of philosophy."[22]

The fourth critique of analytical philosophy is that, despite its general disdain for metaphysics, it has a hidden metaphysic. This criticism seems often true in the case of individual philosophers. As David Pole puts it, "a metaphysic is easier to disown than to disengage oneself from."[23] It is doubtful, however, that this proves anything more than that some analysts have been guilty of special pleading. It has not been demonstrated that the method of linguistic analysis implies any particular metaphysic. It would seem that the method is compatible with several metaphysical positions and perhaps with none at all. It will take a better critique than has yet come forth to prove that linguistic analysis hides, as did logical positivism, a particular metaphysic. And the fact remains that linguistic analysis is one of the best tools for detecting a hidden metaphysic in anyone's thought, including that of the linguistic analyst himself.

In conclusion we note that the thrust of analytical philosophy has made a real penetration into several other disciplines. The sciences in general have paid considerable attention to it. It is common to find academic science departments requiring their majors to take courses in this philosophy. It has begun to influence political and educational philosophy. Perhaps more significant, it is beginning to influence the humanities. We find one British school of poetry under its influence.[24] Novels have appeared that show its influence.[25] This growing influence on other disciplines means that analytical philosophy is making a widening impact upon our culture.

It is obvious that, whether it is the final savior of philosophy or but another halting step along the way, analytical philosophy is making a contribution to thought. It has vitality and represents an important segment of our intellectual culture. Only by engaging in serious conversation with it can we weigh more accurately its potential contribution to theology and other disciplines.

NOTES

1 See Norman Malcolm, *Ludwig Wittgenstein: A Memoir* (London: Oxford University Press, 1958), p. 1.

2 *Ibid.*, p. 15.

3 W. Barrett and H. D. Aiken, *Philosophy in the Twentieth Century*, Vol. 2 (New York: Random House, 1962), p. 486.

4 The biographical facts in this paragraph come from Norman Malcolm, *Ludwig Wittgenstein: A Memoir.*

5 Ludwig Wittgenstein, *Philosophical Investigations,* transl. by G. E. M. Anscombe (New York: Macmillan Company, 1953), p. 3.

6 *Ibid.*, p. 8.

7 *Ibid.*, p. 11.

8 *Ibid.*, pp. 39, 45–46.

9 *Ibid.*, p. 224.

10 *Ibid.*, p. 19.

11 See, for example, Ernest Gellner, *Words and Things* (Boston: Beacon Press, 1959), pp. 30–37.

[12] L. Wittgenstein, *The Blue and Brown Books* (New York: Harper & Brothers, 1960), pp. 27–28.

[13] L. Wittgenstein, *Philosophical Investigations,* pp. 11–12.

[14] L. Wittgenstein, *The Blue and Brown Books,* p. 28.

[15] L. Wittgenstein, *Philosophical Investigations,* p. 168.

[16] D. Pole, *The Later Philosophy of Wittgenstein* (London: Athlone Press, 1958), p. 92.

[17] Quoted by J. O. Urmson, *op. cit.,* pp. 170–171.

[18] L. Wittgenstein, *Philosophical Investigations,* p. 111.

[19] Mary Warnock, *Ethics Since 1900* (London: Oxford University Press, 1960), p. 170.

[20] See, for example, H. Shapley, *Science Ponders Religion* (New York: Appleton-Century-Crofts, 1960), pp. 30, 88–89.

[21] A. G. N. Flew (ed.), *Logic and Language,* 1st series (Oxford: Basil Blackwell, 1955), p. 101.

[22] Quoted by A. G. N. Flew in A. G. N. Flew (ed.), *Essays in Conceptual Analysis* (London: Macmillan & Co., 1956), p. 16.

[23] D. Pole, *op. cit.,* p. 102.

[24] See Paris Leary, "The Movement in England," *The Beloit Poetry Journal,* Vol. 8, No. 2 (Winter 1957–58), 20–22.

[25] For example, see Gabriel Fielding, *In the Time of Greenbloom* (New York: William Morrow & Company, 1957).

4
ANALYTICAL PHILOSOPHY AND THEOLOGICAL LANGUAGE

Our purpose is to examine theological communication in light of a conversation with analytical philosophy, particularly linguistic analysis. Before we can do this, it is necessary to see what this philosophy has said about theological language. Until recently this was little. The logical positivist swept theological statements under the carpet with other "metaphysical" statements but said little to illuminate theological language. In actual practice theology and philosophy had less relationship to each other during the rise of analytical philosophy than they have had since the time of the early Church Fathers. Theologians turned in disdain from thinkers who branded theology as nonsense, and analytical philosophers contemptuously ignored theology or used it to illustrate logical errors.

It is noteworthy that in recent years the gulf between philosophy and theology has been crossed by both linguistic analysts and theologians. A steadily growing group of books has appeared to relate the two fields. Until recently the initiative seems to have been with the philosophers rather than with the theologians. This was due partly to the appearance of Christians among the analysts. It is due also to the greater catholicity of linguistic analysis, which believes that philosophy must analyze language as it is actually used, and certainly theological statements appear in common usage. It is not unusual to find a linguistic analyst who explains that, while he has no concern with religion, he finds theological language fascinating as a producer of problems and puzzles. But whatever the motivation, the analyst no longer ignores theology.

At first the theologian found himself bewildered by analytical philosophy. As Basil Mitchell puts it, traditionally theologians and the general public had thought of the philosopher, like the theologian, as having a pulpit.[1] From this pulpit he expounded his views on the nature of the universe, the really real, and the good life. The theologian might find the philosopher an ally or a rival, but at least he knew what he was doing. The modern philosopher, however, has stepped out of the pulpit, he insists that he has no desire to remake the world or man, he has nothing to preach. He is a critic of language, not a builder of world views.

Formerly the theologian had expected tension between himself and the philosopher. Philosophy was seen as an aid to theology when it provided "proofs of God," but it became a threat when other philosophers attacked the "proofs" and interpreted the world without reference to God. Even when the philosopher produced proofs of God, some theologians were ungracious enough to ask if the God of the philosophers had anything to do with the God of Abraham, Isaac, and Jesus Christ. But despite tension, theologian and philosopher felt a strange kinship because they shared so many interests and concerns.

With the rise of analytical philosophy the scene changed. It was no longer a question of debating whether or not the proofs of God were valid. Now the question thrust forward by philosophy was "Is there any meaning to language about God?" You can debate with the man who denies that you have sufficient evidence for your argument, but how do you talk with the man who finds no meaning in what you say?

At first theologians felt that they did not need to take seriously a philosophy that denied meaning to theological statements. But, as we have seen, theologians are becoming acutely aware of the problems faced in communicating the Christian faith to modern man. Could it be that the philosopher is making explicit the problems that face the man on the street?

In order to understand analytical philosophy's critique of theological language we need to see what it means by calling something "nonsense." An illustration frequently used is that of a man who says he has a fairy that lives in and operates his wristwatch. This seems like a straightforward statement. He means that he has a little intelligent creature that lives in his watch and operates it somewhat as an engineer operates a locomotive. But supposing that, having asked why he believes this, we find that he has never seen the fairy—it is invisible. He has not heard it speak; it does not wind his watch for him or repair it when it is out of order. We begin to realize that his statement about the fairy in his watch tells us nothing about his watch. He is not claiming that his watch differs in any way from watches that do not have fairies in them. There is nothing being claimed that would tell us how to verify or falsify his statement.

In some senses statements about his fairy are meaningful. They are not nonsense in the way that nonsense verse is. If the man holds the watch and speaks lovingly to the fairy, we would say, "He really does believe that there is a fairy in there." This indicates that he has communicated something to us. But what has he communicated? He has told us nothing about the watch, but he has told us that he is the kind of man who believes he has a fairy in his watch. This is why logical positivism called such statements "emotive." They do not give information about the world: they reveal the feelings of the speaker.

The reader can see from this "fairy tale" how philosophers might be inclined to treat theological statements. But we have from John Wisdom the well-known article "Gods," in which he applies this principle to theological language.[2] Wisdom begins by noting that the question of God's existence is no longer an experimental issue as it once seemed to be. We no longer have controlled experiments to prove which God exists, as Elijah did on Mount Carmel. What then is it that the theist sees in the world that is not seen by the atheist? He suggests a parable of a garden which, when revisited, has a few flowers growing vigorously. One observer says that a gardener has been looking after it, for he sees signs of attention, care, and a sense of beauty. Another observer says that if someone were looking after it, there would not be so many weeds. They ask questions and find that no one has seen a gardener, so the believer postulates that the gardener is invisible. The believer in the gardener and the unbeliever continue to examine the garden. Sometimes they find evidences of purposeful care and sometimes they find the opposite. They are completely agreed on the facts of the garden itself; they differ only in that one believes that it is the work of an invisible gardener and the other does not. They do not differ in belief about the garden but rather in how they feel toward it. How can we say that one or the other is right? How can we say that one is more "reasonable" than the other? When all the facts are agreed upon, how can there still be a dispute about the facts?

Wisdom suggests some other arguments where similar features may be found. In a law court we sometimes have disputes where the facts are agreed upon. For example, given the facts, we still can ask, "Was reasonable care exercised?" In such cases the facts are gone over to bring out significance, but there can be no experimental deciding of the case. Or there is the case where two people see the same picture, and one says that it is beautiful and the other says that it is not. They both see the same picture with the same facts, and they try to point out to each other what is significant for their viewpoint. There is no factual dispute, yet there can be a settling of it as one comes to see it in a "new light." Cases in which there are no factual disputes can be argued—they have a form of logic. We can compare them with other cases. As Nathan drove home a point to David about his guilt by telling a parable, so we may get another person to see the facts in a new light.

Wisdom's article leaves the theologian only partly disturbed. It would seem that perhaps statements about God are better off than statements about a fairy in the watch. One feature is clear in Wisdom's parable—he is thinking about natural theology alone. There is no hint that the gardener might have taken the initiative to make himself known. The parable would have taken on some interesting differences if Wisdom had allowed the invisible gardener's son to appear in the garden.

Wisdom's parable is taken over and sharpened by Flew.[3] In his version Flew suggests various stratagems, all unsuccessful, to find empirical evidence of the gardener. But none of this daunts the believer, who still insists that there is a gardener. Finally Flew's skeptic cries, "Just how does what you call an invisible, intangible, eternally elusive gardener differ from an imaginary gardener or even from no gardener at all?"[4] What is happening, says Flew, is that a fine hypothesis is being killed by a thousand qualifications.

To illustrate this, Flew concentrates on the statement "God loves us as a father loves his children." This seems meaningful, but we see a child dying of inoperable cancer and his earthly father is frantic to help but is unable to save his child. The heavenly father, who is presumably omnipotent, does nothing. What does it mean to say that nonetheless God loves the child as the father does? The theologian rushes in with a qualification. God's love is "an inscrutable love." Finally Flew asks: What is the assurance of God's love worth? What could happen to convince the believer that God does not love? If God's love is compatible with any set of facts or conceivable set of facts, then what can it mean? Has a real statement been made?

In one sense Flew is raising the question of pain and evil that is older than the Book of Job or the Psalms. But here the question comes in a new form. We are not asked to justify the ways of God in a few sentences, but we are asked what we *mean* by saying that God is loving. If we say that it is an analogy to speak of God as a father, we must say where the analogy holds. If there is nothing to indicate that God's love operates like a father's love, why call it love? If it is an inscrutable love, how inscrutable can it get? Have we made so many qualifications that it is no longer different from saying that God hates man? What state of affairs have we denied as being the opposite of God's loving man?

Perhaps the philosopher here speaks for the plain man. When a family stands in the midst of tragedy their real question often seems to be the same as Flew's. They want to know, "What do you mean by saying that God loves when he lets this happen?" This is not just a question of a sophisticated skeptic—it comes from man's heart.

To understand Flew's point we might take the statement "All crows are black." We could never prove this absolutely, for even if every crow discovered to date has been black, we could not be certain that the next crow we see will not turn out to be an albino; we would consider the statement a well-established empirical hypothesis. But let us suppose that we found an albino bird hatched by a crow from an egg that it had laid. Since it takes only one case to disprove a universal statement, we would assume that this proved that not all crows are black. But suppose that someone continued to make the statement, arguing, "All crows are black; this bird therefore is not a crow." Now we see that the man has not made a statement about the color of certain birds; his statement "All crows are black" is a definition of how he is using the word "crow." If we make the statement that "*P* is a state of affairs," it logically follows that "not-*P* is not the case." If, when faced by not-*P*, we persist in affirming *P*, it is evident that we are not speaking about any state of affairs.

When Flew turns to theological statements such as "God loves man as a father loves his children," they seem to be vast cosmological assertions. They could not be absolutely proved any more than we could absolutely prove that all crows are black. But, says Flew, if they are assertions, there must be something that they deny. The difficulty with theological statements, argues Flew, is that we cannot find out what they deny. What would have to happen to entitle us to say that God does not love us or that God does not exist? If the believer allows no event, such as the child's dying of cancer, to disprove his statement, then the statement is as empty as the statement of a man who keeps saying that all crows are black after he is shown an albino crow.

Similar considerations lead other analytical philosophers to argue that "God" is a strange subject of any sentence. While the predicates of statements about God seem quite familiar, when "God" is the subject of the sentence the predicates are "traveling in strange company." When we say that God loves as a father loves his children, the word "love" has to be qualified. The same is true when we make "God" the subject of verbs like "wills," "acts," "is angry," "forgives," and so on. In such cases God's activities are not the same as those of a man who would be described by the same words.

But not only does the word "God" cause the predicates to seem strange, it is a strange word itself. To begin with, it looks as though it were the proper name of an individual. But who is the individual? We cannot take someone and introduce him to God as we would introduce him to John Jones. We cannot point to any work that is God's work alone, for everything to which we point has its own causal history which science, history, etc., can describe without any reference to God. If we say that God is found in all that is, it becomes impossible to identify God with anything in particular. As I. M. Crombie puts it, "God" might be called an "improper proper name."[5] The word "God" does not point to the individual of whom it is the name in the way in which proper names are meant to point.

We are finite men living in a finite world, and our language has grown up in our interactions with this finite space-time world. In theological statements we try to take these space-borne words and apply them to one who is beyond all finite affairs, to one who is not a creature but the Creator, not a finite being but the Infinite Being. In such a situation can we still claim any meaning for our language? When I say that John built a house, there are a number of states of affairs to which I may be referring, but the statement delimits a definite set of actions. But to say that God created the universe does not mean, as Augustine saw, that he built it as a carpenter builds a house. Does it then mean anything?

The problem is intensified when we find professional theologians affirming that God's creation of the world is not a hypothesis to be put into competition with scientific hypotheses about the beginnings of the universe. As Langdon Gilkey puts it, "Almost all contemporary theologians would . . . agree that any scientific hypotheses about *how* the universe developed to its present state . . . are equally compatible with this theological affirmation."[6] This may sound startling to popular religion, although it would not have seemed strange to the professional theologians through the ages. But if this is so, argues the philosopher, what kind of statement is "God created the world." If it is compatible with any scientific theory, is it not like claiming all crows to be black after an albino crow has been found?

Of course such difficulties are not new. Down through history theologians have developed ways to meet them. For example, there is the *Via Negativa,* which has been associated with mysticism. It claims that we can make only negative statements about God. We cannot say what God is, we can only say what he is not. The philosopher would admit that negation is a way to point to something. If we have a list containing *X,* we can point out *X* by crossing off all the other items on the list. But, argues the philosopher, God is not an item on the list of the theologian who uses negation. When he crosses off everything that is not God, he is not left beholding the naked face of God, he is left with nothing. If there is nothing that we can say God is, then we cannot even say what he is not.

Another theological method, developed particularly by Thomism, would argue that we can speak of God by analogy. There is an analogy between the being of God and the being of the world. Because God is the Final Cause of the world, the world, as effect, bears an analogy to its Cause. Obviously argument from analogy is useful. If we know that two entities, *X* and *Y,* have in common the characteristics *a, b, c,* and if we know that *X* also has the characteristic *d,* then by analogy we can assume that *Y* also has the characteristic *d.* But such argument is precarious. As logician M. C. Beardsley says, it ought to be restricted to illustration, clarification, and as a suggestion for new possibilities. It cannot be used to prove such things as that *X* possesses the characteristic *d*.[7]

Analogy is precarious because even slight differences between *X* and *Y* can lead to major differences in their characteristics. But when we try to speak of God by analogy, we have already admitted that there is an infinite difference between God and any creature. How then can we know where analogy is valid? Furthermore, analogy can be used legitimately to illustrate and clarify only if we have considerable nonanalogical knowledge of similarities between *X* and *Y*. If we have no nonanalogical knowledge of God, how can we know what analogies are applicable to him?[8] It seems to the philosophical critic that the resort to analogy by theology hides the very problem analogy was meant to solve.

These are not the only objections one finds to theological language in linguistic analysis.[9] But we should not suppose that linguistic analysts are unanimous in denying meaning to theology. Philosopher C. B. Martin says: "The time is now past when philosophers could feel justified in dismissing religious language as 'nonsense' and 'meaningless.' . . . There is still left the task of examining as sympathetically and as critically as possible just *how* religious utterances are used to mean whatever they may mean."[10] But this summary will give an idea of the kind of challenge that must be faced if language is to be used to communicate Christian faith. Furthermore, while it may be objected that these are highly technical considerations, they are often making explicit problems that are implicit in the minds of many today. Any theology that is concerned with the problem of communication must face these problems.

One of the obvious problems in analyzing theological langauge has been that when philosophers have undertaken it they have usually failed to show any deep understanding of theology. The believer can easily object that what has been analyzed is not what he says but a caricature of what he says. On the other hand, when theologians have approached the task of analyzing their language, they seldom have had the logical training to do the job in a fashion to satisfy the philosopher. Here, it would seem, is the role in which philosophy of religion might make a contribution. Unfortunately, few philosophers of religion have made any effort to incorporate the insights of linguistic analysis. Among the philosophers of religion who have used analytical philosophy is Willem Zuurdeeg. Zuurdeeg declares that the task of philosophy of religion is to analyze religious language.[11] A summary of the relationship between analytical philosophy and theology would not be complete without a brief summary of this thought.

The key to Zuurdeeg's position is his concept of "convictional language."[12] He uses the terms "conviction," "convicted," and "convictor" in a technical way which he is at pains to clarify. "Conviction" is chosen for Zuurdeeg's purpose because of its Latin root, *convinco* which means "to overcome, to conquer, to refute." Zuurdeeg develops this technical terminology because he wants a term that will be a better description of what logical positivism called "emotive language." The word "emotive" carries a connotation of unimportance and subjectivism. To call a man's argument "emotive" is to insult him. But Zuurdeeg is not simply trying to find a word with better psychological appeal. "Convictional," he argues, is more descriptive of what is involved. It brings out the fact that the man who speaks of his God, of right or wrong, or of something beautiful, is not describing how he feels, he is pointing to that which has "convicted" him. What the conviction is cannot be a matter of personal taste: it depends on the nature of the "convictor." Christian faith is radically different from Moslem faith, not because Christians emote differently from Moslems, but because of the differences in their convictors.

Zuurdeeg uses the word "conviction" to mean all persuasions concerning the meaning of life, good and bad, gods and devils, ideals, and so forth. Convictions are "sufficient grounds for action." From convictions decisions are made and life is governed. Convictional attitude is *sui generis*. Whereas mathematical certitude and scientific certitude persuade the mind, convictional certitude moves the whole of life.

The convictor is that which has power to overwhelm and overawe. It draws irresistibly. The convictor is normally presented through the "witness" of those who have been convicted, and to the convictor, so presented man makes his response. And yet this response is one in which the power of the convictor is as operative as the will of the one being convicted. The "grounds" of the conviction include the power of the convictor who has come from outside oneself, the witnesses who have pointed to the convictor, the "goods" that are at stake, including a whole way of life, the threat to these goods, and the promise of a new way of life that will come to the convicted.

When a man is convicted he undergoes a radical change in the whole of his life. He has been "converted"; he is a new man. This is equally true whether he is convicted from naturalism to Christianity or vice versa. In a real sense a man is what he says in convictional language. Even though analytical philosophy claims to study language alone, language is never an entity by itself. To study language we must study "man-who-speaks."[13] Man speaks convictional language to establish his existence, to find out who he is. To understand such language it is not sufficient to analyze its logical structure; we must identify who said it, in what circumstances, and what the man was trying to say with the language.

It is impossible for man to live without convictions, although he may be converted from one convictor to another. A man may be unaware of his convictions. The Western world had been living by a host of convictions that were not recognized until the challenge of Nazism appeared. Furthermore, a man is seldom convicted by only one convictor. But we can refer to a region of convictors which usually has a structure and a hierarchy. One convictor normally takes precedence over the others. Where there is a sharp conflict between the convictors in one's life there is a split in one's personality.

From this analysis it is apparent that we cannot say that empirical language deals with "reality" whereas convictional language does not. Convictional language is as much concerned to point to reality as is empirical language. Whether the reality referred to exists, or not, is not a question that analytical philosophy could decide in view of its own concept of philosophy. Convictional language aims to deal with "the whole of reality," whereas science confesses that it deals only with certain relations between certain kinds of facts, that is, with a part of reality.

No language can be free from convictions. In science we must extol objectivity because only by objectivity can science achieve its goals. But this does not mean that scientists are without convictions. The proper place for such convictions is in the presuppositions of the science. Thus to call science "objective" is misleading; it would be better to call it "intersubjective." Actually, if the desired "objectivity" is to be gained, men must be convicted that impartial science is necessary for the good way of life.

We cannot find some realm outside all convictions from which we can weigh the merits of one another's convictions. What we can do is to listen to others' convictions and witness to our own with the faith that what has convicted us has the power to convict others. Through empathy and imagination we can understand the convictions of others, which is a prelude to real dialogue between convictional positions.

Space will not allow us to follow Zuurdeeg further to see how he illustrates and defends his thesis. But he has made an important contribution to our understanding of language. In light of it, for example, we can understand the logical positivist. When the logical positivist claimed that statements lacking logical or empirical verification are meaningless, he was expressing his convictions. He had been convicted by his life and experience that there is no worthwhile reality beyond the space-time world, and he was convicted that, for the preservation of the values he held most dear, he must win people to act on the assumption that reality is exhausted by the space-time world. Furthermore, Zuurdeeg's analysis will alert us to watch for convictional elements in the philosophy of other analysts who claim that their analysis is purely objective. Thus Iris Murdoch chides her fellow analytical philosophers because their analysis of the meaning of ethical language is restricted to the Protestant liberal form of ethics dominant among Anglo-Saxon intellectuals.[14] In Zuurdeeg's terms, their convictional basis has colored their analysis.

Such is the philosophy that has broken into the twentieth century with a philosophical revolution. It has presented a new challenge to theological language; yet in many ways it is an old challenge in a new form. What is theology's response? There seem to be four different approaches that theology might use.

Its first response might be to ignore analytical philosophy in all its forms. This is what most theologians have done until recently. This seems obscurantist, but a case can be made for it. Analytical philosophy is pretty much restricted to professional philosophers, and philosophical schools have their day and disappear. If we ignore the analysts, we can expect to wake up one day and find they are gone. In the meantime what does Jerusalem have to do with this latest outburst from Athens? If a man has lived by a faith and known the power of God's grace, he is not likely to drop his faith just because a philosopher finds that the faith does not fit the categories the philosopher wishes to impose. The believer will reply, with Pascal, that the heart has its reasons which the reason cannot know.

This response, however, seems to miss the basic point. We agree that analytical philosophy is largely the property of professional philosophers, although we have seen that it is spreading to other fields of human thought. And we agree that a man does not abandon his faith because of someone's philosophical doubts. But the problem is not to save the faith of the convinced Christian: it is to communicate with the unbeliever. When we try to tell someone about our faith we must take cognizance of the questions raised in analytical philosophy. We must agonize over the analyst's question "But what do you mean?" This is not simply a matter of speaking to an esoteric group of philosophers, for analytical philosophy is in many ways a sophisticated expression of the type of question that haunts a large proportion of the public today. In an age of scientific prestige, of mechanical wonders, of the unending search for more material luxuries, what is the meaning or the relevance of this "talk about God"? In fact, even children raise theological questions which, despite naïveté of expression, are in essence the same questions raised by analytical philosophers. A theology that takes seriously its task to preach the Gospel to all the world cannot ignore analytical philosophy.

The second response or approach of theology to analytical philosophy is to admit that theological statements are not cognitive, but to insist that they are vital for life because of their emotional, motivational, or other qualities. Theology makes no claim to describe reality, it expresses attitudes and responses. Theological language might be viewed as the poetry of life and, if so, it would be no more fitting to verify theology than it is to verify "Oh, my luve is like a red, red rose."

For those who believe that religion is more than poetry, R. B. Braithwaite has another defence of religion within the framework of the second approach.[15] He argues that both religion and ethics are declarations of policy for behavior. In religion behavioral policies are associated with certain "stories" or "myths." It is an empirical fact that these stories assist individuals to carry out their ethical ideals. It is not necessary, however, that the "stories" be "true," for religion is not intended to tell about reality: it is an inspiration to live a certain way of life.

The second alternative is a tempting way out for the theologian. Even logical positivists admitted that religion might serve an important function as the poetry of life. If we take this alternative there can be no conflict with philosophy. Furthermore, this has the advantage that the simple believer can go on believing theological statements to be true, while the sophisticated theologian "demythologizes" them. And yet we have the uncomfortable feeling that we must not let this information reach the masses. It is, as Braithwaite argues, an empirical fact that religions have inspired men to ethical living. But is it not the case that they have done so because they were believed to be true in some sense? Once no claim of truth is made for them, can they still inspire and motivate men?

The basic problem with this second approach is that it is not an adequate analysis of how, in fact, theological language is used. It is true that the person who makes theological statements normally does reveal something about his own attitudes and behavioral policies. To say that "God created the universe" is to imply a positive attitude towards the universe. To say that "God was in Christ" implies a desire on the part of the speaker to live a Christ-like life. But down through the centuries Christians have not used such statements solely to express attitudes or behavioral policies. They have used them to express belief about reality. Furthermore, Christians have believed that there is a close relationship between the truth of the statement and the attitudes and behavior that normally accompany belief in the statements.

Actually this second approach is not an analysis of how theological statements are used, it is a program for a radically new use of such language. In presenting our own position, it will become more clear why we cannot accept this approach. Here we may simply note an objection made by both believers and non-believers. Even if we believe that the time has come when the truth of theological statements cannot be accepted, would it not be more honest and less confusing to use statements to express attitudes and behavioral policies that have not been traditionally associated with truth claims?

If we are not willing to concede that theological statements make no truth claims, we may turn to the third alternative. The theologian may claim that his statements are meaningful because a rational examination of the universe can verify them. With natural theologians in general, theology will claim that, by an appeal to facts and reasoning open to all rational men, it can demonstrate the truth of Christian belief. Whether it makes use of the classic proofs of God or whether it finds new methods, it will claim to verify theological statements without reference to the particularities of any revelation.

There is much to commend such an approach. The best way to refute analytical philosophers who deny meaning to theological statements would seem to be to demonstrate that the hypothesis that God is the Creator and Governor of the world is at least probable, and perhaps the most probable hypothesis. Furthermore, asks the natural theologian, how else can we approach the unbeliever? If we cannot show him that belief in God is rationally acceptable, if we cannot start with his present experience and lead him, by reason, to accept the existence of God, how can we expect him to listen to a revelation from a God in whom he does not believe? Common reason is the point of contact with the unbeliever that may bring him to the threshold of faith. Thus we can answer the analytical philosopher and solve the problem of communication at the same time. Natural theologians do not deny that faith has its place in religion, but they assert that they can lay a foundation in reason before faith is required.

Despite its appeal, there are serious problems in this approach. We shall indicate, as we proceed, why we cannot accept this position, but we can note here that the philosophers have not been persuaded of the validity of the natural theologian's verification.[16] Since the time of Kant and Hume it has been doubted that human reason could go from the space-time universe to that which transcends space and time. Analytical philosophers have increased this doubt by demonstrating the logical jump that is always involved in such attempts. The arguments appear innocent enough. They begin with familiar concepts, such as cause, design, and moral order. But as they progress these common terms take on new and strange connotations. They become First Cause, Designer of the Universe, the Foundation of Morality, etc. Because of this shift in meaning, it cannot be claimed that the arguments are logically persuasive; their meaning has become dubious. As a result it is argued that the existence of God cannot be considered a legitimate hypothesis to explain anything in the universe or the universe as a whole.[17]

It is evident that natural theology to date has not out-argued the analytical philosophers. Whether it will, remains to be seen. But the fact that we have to wait shows something strange in the natural theologians' approach. Certainly religious faith does not have to wait for the debate to be resolved. Furthermore, it is apparent that a major reason why natural theologians do not persuade analytical philosophers is that they begin from radically different premises and assumptions. It begins to appear that the natural theologians' argument persuades only those who, in Zuurdeeg's terms, share a common convictional framework. Of course, no one has found a method to persuade everyone of the truth of his convictions, but the natural theologian has claimed that he can make his case without going beyond what can be seen by all rational men. But, in fact, he does not go beyond what can be seen by all rational Thomists, idealists, Whiteheadians, and others.

The fourth approach to analytical philosophy is suggested by linguistic analyst J. J. C. Smart. After showing fallacies in natural theology's classical proofs of God, Smart says, "In my opinion religion can stand on its own feet."[18] That is, over against natural theology, which seeks a basis for religious belief outside religion, in "pure reason," Smart is arguing that religion has within itself the ability to persuade. In Wittgenstein's terms, theology has its own language game.

The fourth approach recognizes that what you can persuade any man to believe through the use of reason will be limited by the convictional framework the man holds. This is why natural theology does not persuade all men. In meeting the challenge of analytical philosophy the fourth approach will use the tools of analytical philosophy to detect the convictions, often hidden, in any analysis of theological language. This approach will not attempt to argue within the framework of a convictional pattern alien to Christian convictions. Instead it will witness to Christian convictional premises. As Smart sees, religion speaks "of *conversion,* not of *proof.*"[19]

We can illustrate our point by analyzing philosopher William Blackstone's discussion of religious knowledge. Blackstone begins by admitting, in the fashion of linguistic analysis, that "there are many different uses of 'know.' "[20] He points out that to judge whether a statement constitutes knowledge we must appeal to criteria which function as a norm for "knowledge."[21] The criteria which constitute a norm cannot themselves "be confirmed as either true or false as can statements which conform to these criteria."[22] If we use the criteria and norm to verify themselves, our argument is circular. We can, however, give "sound reasons" for what we choose as the norm of knowledge. Blackstone is now prepared to point out the norms he uses in arriving at "justified knowledge claims." "These methodological requirements consist in the established canons of inductive and deductive logic."[23] When one makes use of these methods and finds that his beliefs are supported by the data collected and interpreted by these "reliable methods," he is justified in claiming his beliefs to be knowledge. The "sound reasons" he gives for accepting these criteria and norms are the "pragmatic ones" that they have proved useful in practice, they enable individuals to decide what degree of belief they should accord to statements without falling into fanaticism, and they yield a body of logically consistent beliefs.

It is quite possible for a man who takes the fourth approach to analytical philosophy to agree with Blackstone up to this point. But Blackstone now goes on to make a distinction between two kinds of knowledge, "formal" and "factual."[24] It is evident that these are the old logical-positivist categories of a priori and empirical. This becomes evident when he interprets "factual" knowledge as information about the "world" and says that "it includes descriptions and explanations of the phenomena of nature."[25] "Nature" is not defined, but he seems to mean by nature that which is open to scientific study. Blackstone is careful not to suggest that these are the only kinds of knowledge, for then he could be required to defend the metaphysics of logical positivism. But for the rest of his book he argues as though these were the only kinds of knowledge, and his analysis of religious language assumes this hidden premise. But he never gives "sound reasons" for so restricting the forms of knowledge.

It is evident that Blackstone, in Zuurdeeg's terms, holds a convictional base that is not shared by the Christian. The fourth approach to analytical philosophy will not attempt to justify Christianity within the narrow confines that Blackstone's convictional position legislates. Instead it will witness to what the Christian believes are "good grounds" for seeing that knowledge is wider than Blackstone implies.

This fourth method enables us to meet objections like those made by Flew. Flew argues that a statement such as "God loves us as a father loves his children" is meaningless because the believer will allow nothing, such as a child dying of cancer, to disprove it. This statement comes, of course, from the language game of Christian faith. In that game it does not stand isolated as it does in Flew's discussion. On the contrary, it is one of a constellation of statements that must stand or fall together. Flew says that such facts as the child's dying of cancer are not allowed to count against the Christian assertion, but he forgets that Christians always have recognized that suffering and evil count against their belief that God is loving. The Bible agonizes over this problem, and the Church has attempted, in various ways, to comprehend the fact of evil. The Christian clings to his faith, not because he allows nothing to count against it, but because he believes that his evidence for believing in God's love is more compelling than the evidence that counts against it.

The Christian has been met by the love of God in the form of Christ on the Cross. Here he finds the meaning of God's love, and it is a suffering love. God is not as different from the father as Flew would have us think. It is highly significant that Flew never once allows a reference to the Cross to creep into his discussion. And yet no Christian statement of God's love is ever made without the presupposition of the Cross. Furthermore, the Christian, believing in the Resurrection of Christ, is convicted that this life is not the end of the story. The child dying of inoperable cancer would be decisive evidence against God's love only if we knew that it was the final chapter in the story. In the Cross and the Resurrection God demonstrated his ability to transform evil into good. When the Christian says that God loves the dying child as does his father, he is saying that God can transform even this tragedy into good for both the earthly father and his child. This may be false, but it is not meaningless.

It is easy to make nonsense out of any statement if, as Flew does, we examine it outside the language game where it arose and is used. For example, science operates on the basic conviction that nature is an orderly system of causation. And yet we could ask what state of affairs does it deny? When an experiment does not turn out as similar experiments usually do, the scientist does not admit that nature may be capricious. He argues that there must have been experimental error. If we refuse to see the scientist's whole language game, we could cheaply demonstrate that science's belief in the orderliness of nature is empty because nothing is allowed to disprove it. Flew has committed the linguistic analyst's unforgivable sin. Instead of asking how the statement is actually used in the game in which it arose, he transfers it to another game and there finds it meaningless. This is like arguing that field goals are nonsense because there is no place for them in baseball.

Taking the fourth method of meeting analytic philosophy will enable the theologian to draw insights from that philosophy. It is obvious from both the nature of analytical philosophy and this approach that there will be no philosophical contributions to the content of theology. Philosophy will add no items of knowledge about God, nor will it prove Christianity superior to other religions. But it can be of service in helping the theologian to organize the language with which he speaks about his faith. By submitting to the philosophical challenge to state what kind of language game he is playing, the believer is stimulated into an analysis of his language that can help him meet many problems of communication. The following chapters will explore this fourth possibility.

NOTES

[1] B. Mitchell (ed.), *Faith and Logic* (London: George Allen & Unwin, 1957), p. 2.

[2] See A. G. N. Flew, *Logic and Language,* 1st series, chap. 10.

[3] A. G. N. Flew and A. MacIntyre (eds.), *New Essays in Philosophical Theology* (New York: Macmillan Company, 1955), pp. 96–130.

[4] *Ibid.*, p. 96.

[5] See B. Mitchell, *op. cit.*, p. 40.

[6] L. Gilkey, *Maker of Heaven and Earth* (Garden City: Doubleday & Company, 1959), p. 31.

[7] M. C. Beardsley, *Practical Logic* (New York: Prentice-Hall, 1950), pp. 105–109.

[8] See W. T. Blackstone, *The Problem of Religious Knowledge* (Englewood Cliffs: Prentice-Hall, 1963), p. 66.

[9] For a more complete summary of these objections see Frederick Ferré, *Language, Logic and God,* chaps. 3, 5, 6, 9.

[10] C. B. Martin, *Religious Belief* (Ithaca: Cornell University Press, 1959), p. 7.

[11] W. F. Zuurdeeg, *An Analytical Philosophy of Religion* (New York: Abingdon Press, 1958), p. 14.

[12] *Ibid.*, chap. 1.

[13] *Ibid.*, chap. 2.

[14] See D. F. Pears (ed.), *The Nature of Metaphysics* (London: Macmillan & Co., 1957), pp. 110–112.

[15] See R. B. Braithwaite, *An Empiricist's View of the Nature of Religious Belief* (Cambridge: Cambridge University Press, 1955).

[16] See A. MacIntyre, *Difficulties in Christian Belief* (London: S. C. M. Press, 1959), chaps. 6, 7.

[17] For example, see J. Hospers, *An Introduction to Philosophical Analysis* (New York: Prentice-Hall, 1953), pp. 356–366.

[18] See Flew and MacIntyre, *New Essays in Philosophical Theology,* p. 40.

[19] *Ibid.*, p. 40.

[20] W. Blackstone, *op. cit.*, p. 126.

[21] *Ibid.*, p. 127.

[22] *Ibid.*, p. 130.

[23] *Ibid.*, p. 136.

[24] *Ibid.*, pp. 137–138.

[25] *Ibid.*, p. 139.

5

THE NATURE OF A LANGUAGE GAME

We have reached a turning point in our conversation with analytical philosophy. So far theology has been primarily listening. From this point the main burden of the conversation will be shifted to theology. We indicated in the last chapter our thesis that theology forms a particular language game. From philosophy we receive the suggestive concept of different language games. But theology cannot allow philosophy to prescribe the nature of its language game, any more than science has allowed philosophy to dictate the nature of its game. Describing the nature of theological language is a theological task. But before attempting such a description we must pause to consider how a language game is distinguished from other games and study some of the implications of such a distinction.

Although Wittgenstein makes much use of the analogy of "games," he does not provide us with a precise definition of a language game. In fact, he uses his suggestive analogy in different senses.[1] Later linguistic analysts refer continually to the basic concept, with or without Wittgenstein's terminology, but we find few attempts to define fully how language games are distinguished from one another.[2] This is not surprising, for, depending upon the nature of the language games in question, the criteria of differentiation will vary widely. The criteria that distinguish chess from baseball are quite different from the criteria that distinguish chess from checkers or baseball from softball. Inasmuch as it is impossible to list the features which all games possess, so it is impossible to list exhaustively the criteria by which games can be distinguished. But we can give some examples to illustrate how a particular language game may be distinguished from other language games.

First of all, linguistic analysis finds that use is a major means of distinguishing language games. For example, empirical language is used to refer to physical objects and their interrelationships. On the other hand, ethical language is used to express what ought to be and to pass judgment upon acts. Empirical language is used to answer questions like "What are the facts?", "What is in the room?", "Is he healthy?" Ethical language is used to answer questions like "What ought I to do?", "Did he do his duty?", "Is he a good man?"

Secondly, we often find that language games are distinguished by different vocabularies. In empirical language we meet words such as "tiger," "house," "atom," "force," and "dissolves." In ethical language we find a quite different set of words, such as "ought," "guilty," "stealing," conscientious," and "duty."

Thirdly, not only do we have a peculiar set of words in a language game but the words are usually closely interrelated and may be definable only in terms of one another. Empirical words are defined ultimately in terms of pointing ("That is what I mean by 'tiger.' ") and in terms of their relation to one another. *The Shorter Oxford English Dictionary* defines "duty" as "that which one ought or is bound to do." It defines "ought" as "the general verb to express duty or obligation." If one went on to make an exhaustive study of the meaning of ethical terms, he would find similar circularity in definition. This circularity of definition often marks the words that form a particular language game. From this it follows that a mark of a language game is frequently the fact that its basic terms cannot be translated into the terms of another game without loss or distortion of meaning. As G. E. Moore illustrated, we cannot translate an ethical term like "good" into an empirical term like "pleasure" without completely changing its meaning.

Fourthly, language games can often be distinguished by differing methods of verification. Of course there are some games, such as giving commands, to which no verification is applicable. But where verification applies, different games are distinguishable by the presence of different forms of verification. If I say, "There is a pencil on the desk," the statement is verified or falsified by looking at the desk. If a competent person does not find the pencil, I would normally concede that my statement had been incorrect. But if I say, "I have a toothache," and a dentist, having examined my tooth, finds that there is nothing wrong with it, I would not suppose that my statement was thereby falsified. The language game that speaks of pencils has a different means of verification from the game that speaks of aches and pains. Logical positivists correctly saw that ethical statements cannot be verified by the same means as empirical statements. But from this they concluded erroneously that ethical statements cannot be verified at all. In recent years linguistic analysts have attempted to show how ethical statements may be verified by the appropriate methods.[3]

Finally, we see that in many cases different language games are rooted in different "convictional" foundations, in Zuurdeeg's sense of "convictional." In the next chapter we shall pursue this further. Here we note that all empirical verification rests on the conviction that sensory data put us into cognitive relation with significant reality. Similarly, behind the verification or justification of ethical statements lies the conviction of a man that he is obligated, that he has duties. We cannot verify the statement "There is a chair in the next room" to a man who believes that all sensory data are illusions, and we cannot verify "You ought not to steal" to a man who recognizes no obligations in life. In other words, all verification presupposes a convictional framework. A different convictional framework implies a different language game.

In advancing our thesis that theological language forms a particular language game we argue that it displays uniqueness in at least these five features. It has a particular use that is related to man's religious life, worship, and commitment. It has its own vocabulary containing words that are ultimately definable only within terms of one another, such as "God," "worship," "grace," and "sin." And we shall argue that it has its own means of verification based upon its own convictional basis.

When we speak of theology as a separate language game we may seem to be compartmentalizing Christianity. The Christian may protest that his faith applies to the whole of his life, not simply to some isolated part of it. Or, it may be objected, this is to set theology apart from the rest of life and thought so that it will be meaningless to the unbeliever or outsider. These objections are based on a misunderstanding of the nature of a language game.

A recognition of different games does not separate life into isolated and unrelated spheres. A hoe is a quite different tool from a rake, but it does not follow that we need two different gardens in which to use them. As different gardening tools find their place within the practice of gardening, so different language games find their place within life.

For example, when we face a question like "Ought we to continue testing nuclear weapons?" it is important to distinguish the empirical from the ethical questions involved. The presence of the word "ought" makes it clear that this is an ethical question, and therefore we should not expect nuclear physics to answer it. But any attempt to answer such an ethical question must be based upon empirical facts. We need answers to questions such as "How much harm will be done to mankind by fallout resulting from such tests?" "How vital to our defense effort is further testing?" Any attempt to make ethical decisions without asking such empirical questions will result in utopian and irrelevant ethics. Since these are empirical questions, we must go to the experts in nuclear physics and military science for answers. One reason why this problem has been so complex is that experts have not agreed in answering such empirical questions.

We need to distinguish the two language games involved here if we are to avoid hopeless confusion. If we could get complete agreement on the empirical facts from the experts, we should still have to make the ethical decision. We should have to weigh the cost of fallout to mankind against the military advantage to be gained, and there are no empirical scales to perform such a weighing operation. When two men differ in their answers to the question because they disagree on the empirical facts, it is obvious that more empirical investigation alone can decide which man is right. But when men are agreed upon the empirical facts but still differ in their ethical answers, there is no use looking for more empirical facts; their difference is an ethical one alone, and it must be debated in ethical language.

Failure to distinguish the differing contributions of the two games results either in making irrelevant ethical statements without empirical facts or in supposing that nuclear physicists are somehow peculiarly blessed to make ethical judgments. The recognition of the two language games involved in this problem does not divide our life into separate compartments. On the contrary, it opens the way to a truly unified life by preserving us from the idea that such a question can be compartmentalized by handing it over to either nuclear or ethical experts.

From this illustration we can conclude that the recognition of the theological language game in no way isolates theology from the "rest" of life. A few years ago a popular slogan in religious circles was "God is the answer." Several wits asked pointedly, "But what is the question?" Of course, "God" is not the answer to every question. If a chemistry examination asks what elements unite to form water, no one will pass by saying "God is the answer." However, as there is an ethical concern about the effect of fallout, although there cannot be an ethical answer to the question of how much harm fallout will cause, so there may be theological interest in all aspects of life even though theology cannot answer many questions. It was a sad day for theology when certain theologians supposed that theology could answer astronomical or biological questions. But the fact that theology cannot answer such questions does not mean that it has no relation to astronomy or biology.

To recognize theology as a separate language game does not exclude theology from any part of life, any more than ethics is banished from the life of a physicist even though ethics cannot answer questions of physics. However, when we ask about the use of theological language we find a further reason why theological language cannot be isolated. An important use of theological language is to orientate the believer to the whole of life. Thus theological language deals with a man's total commitment. There was a time when this integrating aspect of theology was expressed by saying that theology is the "queen of the sciences." This was a dangerous way of putting it, for it led professional theologians to suppose that they had the right to veto the findings of the other sciences. One of the values of recognizing that theology has its own language game is that it reminds us that not all questions are theological.

Speaking of theology as the queen of the sciences did point up the fact that faith gathers the various concerns of life into a pattern. For example, science cannot discover if or why science is valuable and worth pursuing. Neither can science decide how science ought to be used. And yet these are vital questions which every scientist, as a man, must ask. He needs an overall pattern of life within which he sees his science. Whether or not science developed in the West because of its theological pattern is debatable, but it is obvious that the Judaeo-Christian heritage formed a fitting matrix for its rise. This heritage gave men a concept of a world that is orderly and good (Gen. 1:31). On the other hand, it taught that the world is not itself God or sacred; it is a creation to be used by man (Gen. 1:28). Furthermore, this Christian view of life taught that it is vital to minister to the physical needs of man (Matt. 25:31–46). This view of life and the universe provided an atmosphere that was most congenial to the rise of science. Thus, while Christian faith does not answer any scientific questions, it can give the scientist a perspective on why he is a scientist. In other terms, science can be seen as a Christian vocation.

When we see the use of theological language to give integration and direction to life, it is evident that theology does not operate as just another language game. Perhaps it would be helpful to create a new analogy. Instead of thinking of theology as the queen of the sciences, can we think of it as the Olympic Games? The Olympic Games bring together several different games to be played under a common sponsorship and with common standards, purposes, and ideals. The Olympic Committee does not legislate the rules of ice hockey, and much less does it train a hockey player how to play hockey. But ice hockey takes its place within the total pattern of the Olympics, and its players must meet the Olympic standards. Ice hockey is a separate and independent game that is played outside the Olympics by persons who do not meet Olympic standards and for purposes radically different from those of the Olympics. But hockey can also become an integral part of the Olympic schedule, where it takes on a new meaning.

By analogy, natural science and other language games are separate and independent, with their own questions, rules, methods of verification, and ways of giving answers. But the Christian who is a scientist sees his science as his Christian vocation. His Christian faith cannot answer scientific questions any more than the Olympic Committee can tell a hockey player how to shoot the puck. But the Christian does incorporate his scientific work within his total life as a Christian, as hockey fits into the total Olympic schedule.

All analogies are dangerous. It is important in using this analogy to see that we are not suggesting that professional theologians form the "Olympic Committee." We are using the term "theological language" to refer to all speech and thought about God. Theological language operates in the life of every Christian. The Christian who is a scientist and has to decide how he will cooperate with the nuclear weapons program, will make his decision in the light of his Christian faith. But there is no evidence that professional theologians can provide him with better answers than he can find in his own prayerful responsibility before God.

In the modern world religion is often compartmentalized. During the week a man works as a scientist and accepts evolution. On Sunday he goes to church and accepts the Genesis account of Creation as a verbally accurate account of the empirical facts of Creation. This is made possible by not allowing the science and religion compartments of the mind to get onto speaking terms with each other. Such compartmentalization is widely deplored by both science and religion. Many escape it by allowing one of the compartments of the mind to absorb the other. Thus classical fundamentalism would not accept any scientific finding that was not in accord with its interpretation of the Bible. On the other hand, the more common response in our day has been to make science the dictator which decides what, if any, place religion might have. This attitude came to its ultimate conclusion in logical positivism.

Both compartmentalization and absorption are based on the assumption that there is one set of questions to be answered and thus one use of language. Consequently, if the answers of science and religion differ, one must either split his mind and accept one set of answers at one time and another set at another time, or one must accept either the theological or the scientific answers. The failure to see two language games results in absurdities that compare with an Olympic Committee instructing hockey players how to stick-handle or with hockey players insisting that no game should be allowed in the Olympic schedule unless it is played on ice. When two languages are distinguished, however, the way is open to a mutually beneficial relationship.

We have illustrated our concept of theology as the "Olympic Games" in terms of theology and science. This is partly because scientific language and theological language are two games that frequently have been hopelessly confused from both sides. But the principles involved can be used in examining the relation of theology to any other language game. Recognizing these relations will not solve all the tensions and problems involved, but it will put them into a setting where we may hope for fruitful advance.

When we think of theology as the queen of the sciences, it follows almost inevitably that theology is thought of after the pattern of the sciences in general. Since it is queen, it must produce a suprascientific explanation of reality. Wittgenstein points out that much confusion has arisen from thinking of metaphysics after the pattern of science so that it tries to ask and answer questions in the way in which science does.[4] Theology, considered as the queen of the sciences, almost inevitably strives to become metaphysics in this confused sense. As each of the sciences explains the relationships within its field of study, so the queen of the sciences attempts to explain the relationships between the various sciences. It assumes the right to dictate to the sciences because, seeing the whole of reality, it knows each individual science better than the science knows itself. As each individual science strives to give a systematic view of the reality it studies, the queen of the sciences strives for a systematic view of all reality.

Theology, as the Olympics of life, has a more humble task. It does not pretend to be a suprascientific system with answers to all questions left unanswered by science. It is concerned with another kind of question than is science. It does not offer a systematic explanation of the universe; it is a means whereby man is enabled to live his life with a sense of purpose, direction, and integrity.

To think of theology as the Olympic Games of a man's life means that theology must speak to a man in his total life. It is a mistake to suppose that the Christian apologist must learn physics before he can witness to the physicist or that he must be a specialist in art to speak to an artist. As a matter of human relations, a knowledge of the other's field of specialization can help to establish mutual respect and understanding, but it is not essential to have such knowledge in order to communicate the Christian faith. In fact, before any man can hear the Gospel, he must see that he is more than a physicist or an artist; he must see that his specialization is but one game in the "Olympics" of his life.

It is often argued that, if theology is a separate language game, it is impossible to communicate with the unbeliever. Since it is impossible to translate terms from one game into another without distorting or losing their meaning, there is no logical way to communicate a language game to a man who does not already play the game. It is well to be reminded that it is logically impossible to argue a man into the Kingdom of

God. There is a danger, however, that the theologian who sees this will conclude that there is no way for the Christian to communicate with the non-Christian. This is a typical problem that arises when "language is like an engine idling." Men do learn to use new language games. How is this possible?

Wittgenstein reminds us that to describe a different language game is to describe a different way of life. He also demonstrates that it is life, not philosophy, that teaches us new language games. In light of this, we can see that Christian communication is never purely a matter of logic. The Christian must share with the unbeliever the way of life from which theological language comes. Then, and only then, can he hope to make his language meaningful. It is impossible to persuade a man by logic that he ought not to steal if he has no sense of obligation or duty. Since terms like "ought" and "duty" are not translatable into nonethical terms, the man who has no experience of obligation in his life cannot understand ethical language. Similarly, without the experience of the Christian life Christian theology cannot be made meaningful because it is impossible to translate its terms into the terms of another game without distorting their meaning. Linguistic analysis made a vital contribution to the understanding of Christian communication when it pointed out that language gets its meaning from its use in life. As Wittgenstein points out, if we are in a strange country, with entirely strange traditions, we may master the language but still we do not "*understand* the people."[5] When language is uprooted from the life in which it grows it withers and dies. There is no way to share Christian language without sharing Christian life. There is no way to analyze the language game of Christian theology without analyzing the Christian way of life.

This insight from linguistic analysis should help Christians to avoid a tempting error. Because, as we have seen, the traditional language of the Church sounds strange today, the apologist must translate that language. This is what Christian preaching and thinking has done in every age. As German ethical thinking can be translated into English ethical thinking, so Christians have translated the thought forms of an ancient people into those of the age to which the Gospel was being proclaimed. But it is logically impossible to translate from one language game into another. You cannot translate a "forward pass" into "the catcher's throw to second base." Christian apologists are tempted to try to translate Christian terms into terms of other language games, but when they do this they do not translate: they lose the Christian faith. When he says that Tillich and Bultmann pose the question of whether we must go "post-Christian," Nels Ferré is charging that these men have not translated Christian language into modern speech: they have replaced it by a different language game.[6] To decide whether or not this is the case, it would be necessary to analyze fully the nature of Christian theological language and then to analyze the language of these men. But every attempt to translate the faith runs into the danger that it may end up substituting an alien system for the Gospel.

NOTES

[1] See L. Wittgenstein, *The Blue and Brown Books,* pp. vi–vii.

[2] A good discussion of this problem is found in F. Waismann, "Language Strata," in A. Flew, *Logic and Language,* 2d series, pp. 11–31.

[3] For example, see S. Toulmin, *The Place of Reason in Ethics* (Cambridge: Cambridge University Press, 1958), chaps. 11, 13, 14; P. Nowell-Smith, *Ethics* (Harmondsworth: Penguin Books, 1954), chaps. 5–8; R. Brandt, *Ethical Theory* (Englewood Cliffs: Prentice-Hall, 1959), chap. 10.

The shadow of logical positivism still hangs over this discussion. Seldom do we find the ethical analysts speaking of "verifying" ethical statements. Instead they speak of "justifying," "validating," and "giving sound reasons" for ethical statements. In other words, the analysts still tend to limit the use of "verify" to empirical language in general and to science in particular. It is useful to do this insofar as it emphasizes that we cannot judge the truth of an ethical statement in the same way as we judge the truth of an empirical statement. But in breaking with this custom I feel that I am in harmony with the spirit of linguistic analysis in concerning itself with language as it is actually used. *The Shorter Oxford*

English Dictionary defines "verification" as "the action of demonstrating or proving to be true or legitimate by means of evidence or testimony." According to such normal usage the analysts are talking about the "verification" of ethical statements. If the average man hears that it is impossible to "verify" ethical statements, he assumes that it means that it is impossible to distinguish legitimate from illegitimate ethical statements. I see no better reason to accept the logical-positivist redefinition of "verify" than there is to accept its redefinition of "meaning."

[4] L. Wittgenstein, *The Blue and Brown Books,* p. 18.

[5] L. Wittgenstein, *Philosophical Investigations,* p. 223.

[6] See above, p. 12.

6
THEOLOGICAL LANGUAGE AS A LANGUAGE OF A COMMUNITY OF FAITH

As Zuurdeeg points out, all language has its context; it is spoken in a particular community. We cannot claim completeness for any analysis of language that ignores the community in which the language is spoken.[1] A weakness of much analytical philosophy is that it ignores the persons who speak and the community within which they speak. Language is the tool with which the persons of a community communicate. What distinguishes a community from a herd is the use of language. A common language presupposes a common area of experience. Languages arise in response to the reality faced by men, including the reality of their fellowmen. As men gather into communities they develop their particular languages. When men lose their community, the language dies. Thus, to analyze a language is always to analyze a community. Even the language of science, which excludes all personal references, is nonsensical without the presupposition of the scientific community.

Christian theological language arose within the community of the Church. Because the Church has influenced Western society, much of its language is today the common currency of the culture. When the Church's language is used apart from the context in which it arose, it is always likely to undergo a real, even though subtle, change in meaning. Thus, to arrive at the meaning of Christian language we must take it back to the framework within which it arose. The "paradigm case" of theological affirmations is their use in the Church.

The Church is a community of faith; that is, a common faith welds the Church into a community. At first the divided nature of Christendom seems to require that we speak of "theological languages" because it appears that we have churches rather than a Church. The modern ecumenical movement has cast doubt on such a conclusion, however. Christians from differing traditions often have found more in common than they had expected. Of course there are crucial differences of opinion, but most language games leave room for different opinions. In fact, it is impossible to have a real debate between two parties unless they share a common language game. It will take many more years of ecumenical discussion to answer finally whether or not Christianity's divisions imply a variety of language games. But we shall not go too far wrong if we speak here of theological language as *the* language of the Church.

Theological language arises from the community of faith and its experience. But the Church is a community that is called by its faith to preach its Gospel to the whole world. It cannot be content to speak its language within its own fellowship as might a secret lodge. This means that it must ask how it can speak to those outside the Church. Wherever a community tries to speak to those who do not share the experience upon which the community is built there are difficulties. When the scientist steps out of his laboratory to enlighten the rest of us about his science he faces this problem in an acute way. The theologian finds that the Church faces all of these usual problems plus those that grow from out of the unique aspects of the Christian faith.

When we say that theology is the language of a community of faith, we alienate many in the modern world. Faith is widely held to imply the opposite of knowledge. Where evidence is weak or nonexistent, faith is the only possibility. This understanding was encouraged by the traditional viewpoint of natural theology, which has argued that reason goes as far as possible in gaining knowledge of God, and when reason reaches its limit, faith takes over.

When we turn to the New Testament, however, it is evident that faith means something radically different from this popular concept. In the New Testament faith is seen as a power and a means whereby acts, otherwise impossible, are accomplished (Mark 11:23). Jesus can tell those whom he has healed that their faith has made them well. (Luke 17:19). Faith purifies men's hearts (Acts 15:9), justifies them before God, and brings them into the true relationship with God (Gal. 3:23–26; Rom. 3:28). It makes for righteousness in men's lives (Rom. 1:17). Faith has the power to overcome the world (I John 5:4). Faith is defined as the opposite of sin (Rom. 14:23). Christ himself actually comes to dwell in the life of the believer through faith (Eph. 3:17).

Where faith is defined in terms of the absence of evidence it is logical to assume that in this life we must have faith that there is a God because we do not have enough evidence to know that there is a God. But, in the next life, when we meet God face to face, we shall know that he is, and the time for faith will be past. But Paul tells us that it is knowledge that shall pass away (I Cor. 13:8), while faith will still abide with hope and love (I Cor. 13:13). This statement would be pure absurdity if Paul were using faith in the popular sense that defines it in terms of a lack of knowledge. To the man who thinks that faith logically implies the lack of evidence, Hebrews answers that faith is "the evidence of things not seen" (Heb. 11:1, A.V.). It is clear that for the New Testament writers the word "faith" is used to connote something quite different from its popular use today.

In the New Testament faith is the other side of the coin from the act of God himself. It is never "faith in faith." It always implies faith in God through Christ. Faith will not have power except through prayer, which brings man into the presence of God (Mark 9:29). As E. Stauffer points out, it is the word of the Gospel, proclaiming the acts of God, that calls out faith from men (Rom. 1:16, 10:8; John 4:50).[2]

New Testament faith has much in common with Zuurdeeg's

concept of convictional language. It is interesting to notice that where the Authorized Version translates Hebrews 11:1 to read that faith is the "evidence," the Revised Standard Version translates it to read that faith is the "conviction." This translation helps us to see that faith is convictional language that points to a convictor. In no sense is faith merely emotive or subjective; it is a whole response of the person. It is directed to the object of faith, the Convictor revealed through Christ.

Dorothy Emmet, a philosopher, has shown a real appreciation for the meaning of faith. She points out that faith is "a positive response of the whole nature, involving emotional and volitional as well as cognitive elements."[3] This means, she continues, that the popular defense of faith as a rational act of choosing the most likely hypothesis is completely misleading. Choosing the most likely probability is a purely rational or analytical action. It can be purely theoretical. But faith takes us out of the theoretical attitude. As an example of faith Miss Emmet points to the decision of the British to continue resisting Hitler in 1940. Such a decision was not based on a weighing of probabilities but was a challenge that could not be refused. The British had come to the point where they could only say, "Here I stand, I can do no other, God help me."

The concept of a whole response is further brought out by Miss Emmet when she distinguishes "partial" and "total" assertions.[4] A partial statement points either to a particular fact verifiable by empirical data or to a logical proposition verified by its coherence with other propositions of the same type. (This reminds us of the logical-positivist verification theory.) But a whole statement, such as "He is a good man" cannot be exhaustively analyzed into any number of partial statements. Of course we can make partial statements to justify our use of the term—"He gives to charities," "always tells the truth." But these could never be added up to mean the same thing as saying that he is a good man. In fact, we might accept these propositions as true of someone else and still deny that he is a good man. Miss Emmet quotes Paul's statement that even if he gives all to the poor and his body to be burned and has not love, he is as nothing. In this case the having of love is a total assertion. Similarly to say that a man has faith is to make a total assertion about him.

This analysis helps us to see how the Reformers could speak of faith as a gift. The response of faith is not comparable to assessing a body of facts and making a rational judgment about certain probabilities. On the contrary, in faith we are "grasped" or overwhelmed by the facts. The "will to believe" does not enter into faith. This is why in the New Testament faith and the Grace of God are nearly always joined together. It is God's grace, God's prior act, that makes faith possible. The faithful are properly called the "elect"; they are the ones to whom God has spoken and made possible the response of faith. This brings us close to a doctrine of predestination, and this has been the valid insight expressed by doctrines of predestination. This does not force us, however, into any traditional doctrines of predestination, for man's response to God's grace is his own response. But God's grace is presupposed in the response of faith. Without a convictor (God's grace) there can be no conviction (man's faith).

To call faith "emotive" or "subjective" is a half-truth insofar as it points up the fact that faith implies a decision, a commitment. Faith is trust, as the Reformers saw so clearly. It means putting one's life into the hands of God. If we do not act upon it, it is not faith. But this is only one side of faith. The other side is that faith is a conviction of knowing that is related to a Convictor that comes to us from beyond ourselves and "overwhelms" us. It is being gripped by reality that has awakened faith within us. This aspect of faith makes it misleading to refer to it as subjective or emotive.

Now we must ask if faith can be located logically. Can we analyze the logic of faith? It is often said that Christian faith is unique; it is a *sui generis* act that cannot be located among human activities in general. This may be true, but if so, it is not because of something radically different in the faith response of man but because of the One to whom the response is made. We must not suppose that it is a priori impossible to analyze the logic of faith.

We can locate the logic of faith if we note that, as Wittgenstein says, the giving of reasons must come to an end.[5] When a particular belief is challenged we can give reasons for it. But when we have given all the reasons we can, when we have made all the moves possible in the language game, no more can be done. If someone does not play the game, no further reasoning can force him to do so.

We have criticized the idea that faith is belief on insufficient evidence. But we must note that there is another sense in which we may say that faith means believing without evidence. However, there are two radically different meanings of such a statement. The one, which is rightly deplored, is believing something without regard for evidence. This is not faith in the theological sense. It is wishful thinking, servile submission to authority, and so on. But in any argument there is always something that is accepted without evidence, and that is the evidence itself. What evidence do you have to prove that your evidence is evidence? Sometimes this can be answered. If in a law court a scientific expert's opinion is used as evidence, it is proper to ask what evidence there is to show that he is an expert. But at some point evidence for evidence must cease and the evidence must, so to speak, "prove itself." The acceptance of evidence may properly be called an act of faith.

Linguistic analysis has made a number of contributions to clarify this point. A. J. Ayer, for example, says, "One may be called upon to justify a particular conclusion, and then one can appeal to the appropriate evidence. But no more in these cases than in the case of the more general problem of induction, can there be a proof that what we take to be good evidence really is so."[6] Before saying this Ayer had indicated that we cannot logically justify the principle of induction. All science is built on the assumption that the future will resemble the past; every scientific law hides this assumption. But how can this assumption be verified? It cannot. Even if we say that we accept it because it works so that predictions made on this basis in the past have proven true, it is a reliable argument only if we assume induction and, of course, this makes it circular.[7] But, Ayer argues, this does not make induction or science irrational; rather this is what sets the standard of rationality.

The realm of the a priori is similar. We verify theorems by going back to the axioms in geometry, but if someone denies our axioms, we cannot persuade him. If he accepts the axioms of Euclidean geometry, we can persuade him that the angles of a triangle equal 180 degrees. But if he accepts only the axioms of a non-Euclidean geometry, we cannot so persuade him. In statements of logic we ultimately refer the objector to the dictionary definition of the words to demonstrate that statements are necessarily true, but if he does not accept our dictionary, we cease talking to him.

Does this mean that all thought is ultimately based upon certain arbitrary assumptions? It depends upon the meaning of "arbitrary." Speaking of justifying ethical statements, R. M. Hare points out that the ultimate justification of such statements requires a complete account of their effects and the principles which they observe. This, he sees, means giving a complete account of the way of life of which such ethical statements are a part. If someone demands more justification and asks why this way of life should be considered right or best, there is nothing further that we can say, for we have already given the best kind of justification. We have to challenge the questioner to make his decision. Does he want to be a part of this way of life or not? In our terms, is he convicted by this way of life?[8]

But, Hare continues, this does not mean that our ultimate moral justifications are arbitrary.

> To describe such ultimate decisions as arbitrary, because *ex hypothesi* everything which could be used to justify them has already been included in the decision, would be like saying that a complete description of the universe was utterly unfounded, because no further fact could be called upon in corroboration of it. This is not how we

> use the words 'arbitrary' and 'unfounded.' Far from being arbitrary, such a decision would be the most well-founded of decisions, because it would be based upon a consideration of everything upon which it could possibly be founded.[9]

In a sense all reasoning is like the appeal to set standards. If the government inspector brings his standard weight to test my scales, I may ask whether his standard weight really weighs a pound. This could be answered by comparing his weight with the nation's standard weight. If we ask if this really weighs a pound, we can test it by the international standard pound weight. But if someone asks if this latter really weighs a pound, there is nothing by which to test it. This is, by definition, what a pound is. Of course standard weights are chosen arbitrarily and could be changed if desired. But in other realms of discourse the appeal to the "standard" is the appeal to that which has convicted us, and this, as we have seen, is not to be changed at will. In the deepest sense, we do not choose our convictors arbitrarily or otherwise: we are chosen by our convictors.

One point in analytical philosophy's critique of metaphysics is that often metaphysical questions are comparable to asking if the standard pound really weighs a pound. As such a metaphysical question would be the question that could still be asked when we had all of the evidence before us. It would ask how we know that evidence is evidence. When we ask if sensory data gives us knowledge of reality or if the physical universe is real or if the presuppositions of science are valid, we are asking such questions. To call such questions meaningless is to say that they are unanswerable. We cannot give more evidence than the evidence itself. If, having surveyed the evidence, we remain unpersuaded, reason cannot resolve our doubts.

One reason why men ask metaphysical questions is that they suffer anxiety. No one likes to think that he is being fooled. He wants the truth, the whole truth, and nothing but the truth. Wherever he has doubts he longs to dispel them. If he cannot do so, he feels that the meaning and significance of his life is threatened. Consequently, metaphysical theories take the form of theories about the whole of reality and describe the "really real." What the metaphysician is trying to do is to still his anxious doubt by proving that his dearest hopes and dreams are based on reality.

In light of this interpretation of metaphysics there is a potential value in metaphysics that is often overlooked by its analytical critics. Every age is likely to be living by convictions that certain things are final evidence which in fact may not be final. It is as though the people of a backwoods village had never thought to ask if the scales at their local store really weighed a pound. In such cases a metaphysical probing may bring to light the penultimate nature of that which was assumed to be ultimate. But one thing a metaphysical study cannot do is to operate without an ultimate faith that takes the form of being convicted by a convictor and accepting as evidence that which has the power to convict.

The reason metaphysical questions can be neither answered nor silenced is that, in the last analysis, what really divides men is their concept of what is evidence. The positivist philosopher R. Von Mises notes, "It does not require much speculation to convince oneself of how divided, in all domains, the opinions are as to which statements have the property of evidence."[10] There are persons who seem oblivious of any need to look for evidence, but they are the exceptions. Most men long ago have committed themselves to following where the evidence leads. But this is not the end of disagreement, it is its beginning. For now we face the question of what is evidence. When a man charges that I have no evidence for my conclusions, he may be literally correct, but it is more likely that what he really means is that what I call evidence he does not call evidence.

Dorothy Emmet throws light on this problem with the concept of what she calls "importance."[11] Since "importance" sounds subjective, she notes, it has received scant attention from logicians. But if no one had an interest, based on his conviction that something is significant or important, he could gain no knowledge. The zeal for truth presupposes the importance of what is to be known. Without a concept of importance we would be inundated by facts. Concentration means the ability to ignore those facts that are deemed insignificant in favor of those deemed significant.

As man lives his life in community with his fellowmen he is convicted by his experience that certain things are important. These are the things that are "real." Reference to these becomes evidence for him. This is truly convictional, for man cannot sit down and decide which things will be important to him. In the total context of his life, including the society in which he lives and its convictions, he is convicted by certain features of his environment. In pure logic, a fact is a fact and no fact is more of a fact than any other. But in real life, facts have greatly varying importance. What a society comes to know will depend to a large extent upon what it considers important. If Western culture has advanced beyond other societies in the development of the physical sciences, it is not because the men of this culture have some kind of superior intelligence or scientific aptitude: it is because this culture has seen a much greater importance in the facts of the physical world than have other cultures.

In this view it is obvious that there is a convictional (hence faith) element in most language games. This is true even in the realm of empirical indicative language. The logical positivist was sure that empirical statements are, by their nature, free from "emotive" elements. But are they? We have already seen that logical positivism had a metaphysic in that it claimed that only empirical experience is evidence about reality. But we can go further. All men do not recognize evidential significance in empirical experience. Classical Hindu philosophers and others have argued that such experiences are illusions and, instead of showing us reality, they lead us away from reality.

What is at stake when a logical positivist says that only empirical facts are significant or cognitively relevant and a Hindu philosopher denies that they are either significant or cognitively relevant? The Hindu presumably has the same sensory equipment that the logical positivist has, and he sees, hears, feels, and smells pretty much the same things as does the logical positivist. What divides them is the judgment about the importance of these experiences. To the positivist, sense data put us into contact with the only important reality there is. To the Hindu, they are illusions that lead away from the only significant reality. The Hindu might accept the terminology of the logical positivist, in which case he could say that the logical positivist's statements about empirical experiences are "emotive" statements because they tell only how the positivist sees, feels, and so on. They do not tell us about reality, they tell us only about the speaker.

Here is a typical clash of convictions. Each man is pointing to his convictor. How can we resolve such an argument? Certainly we cannot resolve it by any kind of logic or appeal to the facts, for the argument is precisely over what should be considered "facts." (We might also note that the Hindu would quite likely deny that logic could be useful in knowing the true reality.) To get at true reality the Hindu has his own methods and his own evidence to propose. This is a battle of faith. As F. Waismann has pointed out, the empiricist has a "let-the-facts-speak-for-themselves" *faith.*[12] This is not a faith that the Hindu shares.

In such a debate each man attempts to witness to his convictor in such a way that the other will come to see it for himself. The dream of classical metaphysics, of course, is to provide a rational argument to crush the other's doubt. But there can be no such argument. If the convictor cannot persuade the doubter, nothing can. When someone doubts the objective reality of the physical world, Westerners instinctively want to stick the man with a pin. What is the purpose of such a primitive reaction? Is it not a realization that the material world itself must persuade the man? It is an attempt to get the other to see importance in what he seems to be overlooking. But, of course, it is not an appeal to logic. The unbeliever has no doubts that pins hurt; he too admits to having illusions. The question is not whether the pin hurts but whether it is significant that it does. This explains, in part, why the Hindu trains himself to stand pain, to sleep on spikes, and so on. He is witnessing to his convictor by showing that pains are so insignificant that the man who knows true reality can ignore these unimportant annoyances.

There is no logical or empirical way to resolve the argument between the logical positivist and the Hindu. Therefore, the logical positivist would call the issue nonsensical and meaningless, but the two viewpoints express totally different ways of life. To say that such a debate is "unimportant" is to make a convictional statement. It will be interesting to see how the introduction of Western scientific techniques into India may change the traditional Hindu philosophy. Certainly they cannot logically persuade the Hindu that his philosophy is wrong, but the comforts they bring may convert him to a new concept of importance. If this should happen, it would be a convictional victory, not a rational one.

This excursion around what might be called the limits of rational discourse should help us to locate the logical nature of faith. To say that theological language is rooted in the community of faith, the Church, is to say that the Church is made into a community through the sharing of a certain convictional framework. The Church is convicted that certain events in history have crucial "importance" or significance—they constitute evidence. This is expressed by Jesus when he so frequently says, "He who has ears to hear, let him hear" (Matt. 11:15). That is, not all who hear these things are able to recognize their importance.

We began by indicating that "faith," in its Christian context, means the response of the whole man who, having been convicted by a convictor, commits himself in trust. Next, we examined the convictional element in all claims to knowledge. This did not mean to imply that the convictions involved in all knowledge are identical in form with Christian faith. It was an attempt to find the type of statement to which faith statements belong. Religious language, Christian or otherwise, is unique because it deals with the ultimate convictions of a man's life (his Olympic Games), the convictions by which he lives and dies. Religious convictions decide what in life is supremely worthwhile, what is truly good and real, what we can ultimately depend upon, what we can hope for, to what, or whom, we can say, "Not my will but thine be done." Religious convictions answer the question of why life is worth living. Consequently religious convictions demand the whole of a man in a way that no other convictions do. But, logically speaking, ultimate religious statements can be classified with other statements where man can only refer to the evidence, trusting that the evidence can justify itself. They are convictional statements that point to their convictor.

Speaking of "a convictor" is not meant to imply that there is necessarily one fact or one set of facts that convicts a man. As R. M. Hare pointed out, the convictor in ethical statements is ultimately the whole way of life of which the ethical statement is a part. This does not mean that every time we justify an ethical statement we have to go through an analysis of the whole way of life involved. Most ethical statements are made within a community that shares a relatively wide agreement on what constitutes the good life. Therefore we justify our ethical statements by showing that what we are advocating will bring certain results that are desirable to our consensus. But where we face a real ethical divergence we do ultimately have to go back to the whole way of life involved. Why is democracy better than communism? We have to start listing the features of democracy—freedom, self-government, etc., and someone may object that we are merely describing democracy and that from such "is" statements no "ought" can be deduced. But the point is that what convicts us that democracy is ethically superior is this constellation of attributes. Life in a democracy has convicted us that these are superior ways. If a man sees no value in freedom and the other attributes, he will not be persuaded. All we can do is invite him to come and live with us in the confidence that what has convicted us will convict him.

When the Christian points to his convictor he points to the totality of the Christian way of life. He begins with the foundation of the faith in the "History of salvation"—the chosen people; the life, teaching, death, and resurrection of

Christ; the witness of the early Church through the Scriptures; and the continuing life of the Church through the ages. The Christian also witnesses by telling what this means to his life, how it illuminates and integrates his total experience. He points to the activity of the Holy Spirit. All of this is prelude to inviting the unbeliever to "come and live with him." No man can convert another person to Christianity. He can only expose him to it with confidence that, if the other person will look and listen, God in Christ through the Holy Spirit will convict him. Faith in Christ is the conviction that in Christ we have the evidence that has the power of persuasion to win men. "And I, if I be lifted up from the earth, will draw all men unto me" (John 12:32, A.V.).

In light of this analysis we can look again at the debate that has disturbed theology in our century between the defenders of natural theology and kerygmatic theology. Natural theology, Protestant and Catholic, aims to build a basis for the Christian faith in reason alone. By an appeal to the truths that can be discerned by any rational man the unbeliever is to be brought to the point where he can receive the fruits of revelation. The claim is put forcefully by Henri Renard, S.J., when he says, "The knowledge of the God of philosophy is a scientific knowledge, a knowledge of conclusions which are derived from self-evident principles and factual experience."[13] The natural theologian claims to be able to establish an area of agreement with the unbeliever in the realm of pure reason alone. It is obvious that natural theology does not persuade all men. Does this mean that the unpersuaded are not rational? Some natural theologians are ready to affirm that this is the explanation. Thus Maurice Holloway, S.J., having discussed several other philosophical positions, explains why only Thomists seem to accept his arguments and says, "There are many ways we can be wrong about a thing, but only one way we can be right."[14] However, it must be admitted that many of the unpersuaded are men who would be called "rational" by any other definition of the term. When we analyze why this is so, it is apparent that every natural theology has to make presuppositions about what is evidence and what is important. In other words, it has a convictional basis. The man whose convictions differ from the natural theologian's will not be persuaded.

We see an example of this in Thomism, which takes as a basic premise the proposition that every event or thing must have a cause. Its proofs of God depend upon this, and it is advanced as a necessary truth of reason that man must see if he is rational.[15] But what kind of statement is this? It might be a priori, in which case it is true by definition. Only things that are "caused" would be "events." But if this is the case, it is obvious that the proposition tells us nothing about the world. Thomists cannot continue to reject the ontological argument, as they do, if their own proofs depend upon the same kind of proof by definition that they see as the fallacy of the ontological argument. So it must be meant to be a statement about the world, in which case, being a universal statement, it could not be proved absolutely, but it would be open to disproof. Whether it has been disproved is debatable, but modern science in its quantum theory does not make use of the principle of causality and seems to imply that causality does not apply to subatomic events. As F. Waismann points out, whether the present quantum theory of physics continues to be an accepted theory or whether it will someday be found wanting, its very existence proves that it is possible for rational scientists to conceive of events as having no causes. "Hence every attempt at raising the principle of causality to the status of a necessary truth is irreconcilable with the situation as it has emerged in science."[16]

H. H. Price says that the traditional proofs of God should not be seen as proofs in the sense that they "would follow logically from premisses which every reasonable man is bound to accept," but rather "as analyses or clarifications of propositions which religious persons antecedently believe."[17] Our discussion of convictional language helps us to see why this is so. Reason cannot decide between conflicting convictional claims because every act of reasoning means going back to the evidence. But the question as to what is evidence is precisely what is involved in convictional battles. Those convicted in Thomist circles have intellects that "positively see" certain things and these things become evidence for proving God. But others do not "positively see" such things, they do not see them at all; these things are not evidence, they are illusions or mistakes. It is no accident that the hope of building a natural theology arose in an age that had a widespread agreement on a common convictional pattern.

The kerygmatic theologian, on the other hand, confesses that he begins from faith. He admits that he has been convicted by the revelation of God in Christ and here he finds his ultimate evidence. He seeks to proclaim the message that has come to him in the confidence that it will convict his hearers. Karl Barth says theology so viewed "is always on the narrow way leading from the revelation that happened to the revelation promised."[18]

It is evident that the differences between kerygmatic and natural theology are not of the nature that is at first supposed. Both actually begin from convictions, or faith, and both win agreement only from those who are convicted by the evidence to which they appeal. Natural theology does not proceed from "pure reason," whatever that might be; it operates out of a particular faith, a convictional framework. On the other hand, kerygmatic theology is no enemy of reason; what it denies is that reason by itself can establish convictions. But, given its convictional basis, kerygmatic theology strives to show the meaning, that is, the reasonableness, of the message that comes from God.[19]

If it is recognized that natural theology is not without faith and that kerygmatic theology is not content to be irrational, the two approaches might find some reconciliation. Because kerygmatic theology begins from revelation, it is in danger of phrasing its message in a language that has lost contact with the world in which it finds itself. Since natural theology begins with the world, it may teach kerygmatic theology lessons in communication. On the other hand, natural theology can learn from kerygmatic that a man's reason is always rooted in a convictional frame of reference that determines what is significant or what can be accepted as evidence. When it is a man's convictional framework that renders Christianity impossible for him, he must be converted, not outargued; that is, he must be brought by life to see importance, and thus evidential power, where formerly he has not seen it.

In this discussion we have defined natural theology in its classical form as the attempt to gain knowledge about God that can be discovered by any rational man apart from faith or revelation. This must not be confused with what we may call a "theology of nature." Because theological language operates as the "Olympics" of his life, the Christian will attempt to see his world in the light of his faith. A theology of nature makes no claim to stand apart from its convictions. It is a rational venture, impelled by the nature of faith itself, to "make sense" out of one's world. Such an interpretation of one's world can be a part of witnessing to one's convictor. When Nels Ferré says that we need to rethink natural theology "within the context of incarnational theology," it would seem that he is advocating what we are calling a theology of nature rather than natural theology in its classical sense.[20]

This analysis of the convictional element in theological language helps to clarify another current theological debate. Kerygmatic theologians often argue that natural theology is impossible because sin has corrupted man's reason. Natural theologians reply that this is false. The fact that man is sinful does not mean that he cannot reason well. He still knows that two two's are four, he is as capable of scientific tasks as is the saint. It is doubtful that kerygmatic theologians would argue that sin corrupts man's logical faculties. If that is what they mean, it is obvious that they are wrong. But the judgment of what is ultimately important is a judgment made by the whole man; it is not a matter of pure logic. To say that here man is not affected by sin would be strange indeed. The sinner will have a distorted view of what is truly important. Because the question of God is not a question for man's logic but a question of what is most significant to him, it would seem obvious that, if a man is a sinner, this would prevent his finding God by reason, for his reason's frame of reference would be distorted. If sin causes a man to find primary importance in the wrong facts, his conclusions will be distorted. He "has ears" but he will not "hear."

Many will fear that what is said in this chapter will cast us adrift in a sea of relativism. Since we cannot bring our convictions before the bar of universal reason to see which ones are correct, is not man left in pure relativity? Do we have any defense against the worst of superstitions? We might answer this objection by saying that nevertheless, it does seem a rather good description of the situation. Dorothy Emmet, who is far more friendly to metaphysics than most philosophers today, confesses, "It may indeed be possible that there is some relation or group of relations of adequate generality and applicability to provide a universal metaphysics . . . but, in our opinion, they have not yet been formulated."[21]

But there is a better answer. The assumption that the position outlined here leads to relativism is based on the assumption that our truest knowledge (or even our only knowledge) is what we have at the end of a discursive argument. But, as John Baillie has pointed out, this is not so. When we "reason things out," what we are trying to do is to bring out the grounds for the knowledge we already have and thereby to add further knowledge.[22] If we had no knowledge before discursive arguments, we could not have discursive arguments. Baillie notes that it is common to have knowledge where we are unable to give reasons for having it. He illustrates this by referring to the fact that we have no difficulty in distinguishing the world of our dreams from our waking world. And yet how many, when pressed, can give convincing arguments for this distinction? Astute philosophers can offer quite rational arguments to show that all of life is a dream or that the dream world is the real world. Baillie finds similar examples in our knowledge that it is our duty to help our neighbor or in our knowledge that a particular man is to be trusted. Baillie's point is obviously applicable to what we have described as convictional knowledge.

The inability of reason to verify convictions is not a limitation on their certainty: it is their strength. Convictions are not verified by logical argument: they are the presuppositions of all logical argument. A discursive argument may err in two ways. It may start from false convictions, or its process of logic may be fallacious. But convictions have only one possibility of being wrong—they may be falsely convicted as to what is real and significant.

Finally, we would note that convictional statements are statements that declare something to be ultimately important and hence have the power of evidence. Thus a recognition of the convictional basis of all knowledge does not give a man a free pass to accept all manner of superstitions, such as belief in witches or ghosts. Such beliefs are seldom advanced as convictional. On the contrary, such superstitions usually point to some evidence. Reason can still battle these superstitions by pointing to faulty reasoning or inadequate evidence. Men did not give up their belief in witches because of basic changes in their convictional patterns. They gave up the belief because they were convinced that their conclusions were invalid and that their evidence was insufficient. In most cases they were persuaded by men who shared their convictional patterns.

The truth of all theories of relativism is that man is not infallible. Recognizing this fact, we ought to present our convictions and our conclusions with humility and with a willingness to listen to the convictions and conclusions of others. But the recognition of the convictional basis of all knowledge does not condemn us to relativism any more than does any position which is ready to confess the finiteness of man and his knowledge.

NOTES

[1] W. Zuurdeeg, *op. cit.,* pp. 16–17.

[2] E. Stauffer, *New Testament Theology,* transl. by J. Marsh (New York: Macmillan Company, 1955), p. 170.

[3] D. M. Emmet, *The Nature of Metaphysical Thinking* (London: Macmillan & Co., 1957), p. 139.

[4] *Ibid.,* pp. 141–144.

[5] L. Wittgenstein, *The Blue and Brown Books,* p. 143.

[6] A. J. Ayer, *The Problem of Knowledge* (Harmondsworth: Penguin Books, 1956), p. 81.

[7] *Ibid.*, pp. 74–75.

[8] R. M. Hare, *The Language of Morals* (London: Oxford University Press, 1952), pp. 68 ff.

[9] *Ibid.*, p. 69.

[10] R. Von Mises, *Positivism: A Study in Human Understanding* (New York: George Braziller, 1956), p. 128.

[11] D. M. Emmet, *op. cit.*, pp. 195–197.

[12] In A. Flew, *Logic and Language*, first series, p. 142.

[13] See Foreword to M. R. Holloway, *An Introduction to Natural Theology* (New York: Appleton-Century-Crofts, 1959), p. ix.

[14] *Ibid.*, p. 443.

[15] *Ibid.*, pp. 72 ff.

[16] See A. Flew, *Logic and Language*, first series, p. 133.

[17] Quoted by M. B. Foster in B. Mitchell, *op. cit.*, p. 202.

[18] K. Barth, *Church Dogmatics*, Vol. I, part 1. transl. by G. T. Thomson (New York: Charles Scribner's Sons, 1955), p. 15.

[19] For example see *Ibid.*, pp. 231 ff.

[20] N. Ferré: *Searchlights on Contemporary Theology*, p. 152.

[21] D. Emmet, *op. cit.*, p. 197.

[22] J. Baillie, *The Sense of the Presence of God* (New York: Charles Scribner's Sons, 1962), pp. 60 ff.

7

THEOLOGICAL LANGUAGE AND THE REALM OF MYSTERY

When we analyze theological language we find that it is rooted in a community bound together by a common faith. Faith is identified in terms of appealing to an ultimate convictor, that is, of pointing to evidence that "confirms" itself. We found that, logically speaking, theology shares this characteristic with other kinds of statement. The statement that "the material world is real" is convictional, but it is not theological. We need to see that theology, as the language of the Church, has other features that belong to its "game." In this chapter we shall see that theological language points to a convictor who is known to be a mystery.

Although we are not attempting anything so pretentious as an analysis of religious language in general, we may note that religion is rooted in the experience of the mysterious. Man finds himself face to face with that which convicts him of mystery. When the Christian says that God is transcendent he is using a symbol to refer to the mystery of God. To say that God is transcendent is not to picture the universe as a spatial box with God overflowing it or standing outside it. It is to point to the mystery of God. The same is true when we speak of God as "high and lifted up" (Isa. 6:1). This does not mean that we need a telescope to see God beyond the furthest star; it means that God is the Mysterious One. When a Russian astronaut orbits in space and announces that he did not see

God, it does not surprise the Christian. The astronaut forgot (or never knew) that God is mystery.

Bishop Robinson argues that we need to cease speaking of a God "up there" and "out there," and substitute the concept of God as the "depth" of life.[1] Whether this is a significant contribution to communication is debatable. But we must see that terms like "up there" were never used in Christian terminology to locate God in space. The New Testament knew that God was a spirit and was not to be located on the map (John 4:24, 1:18; Heb. 11:3). In speaking of God as "high and lifted up" Christians have confessed the mystery of God. Possibly another terminology would better express this mystery today. Whatever the language we use, however, it will fail if we do not strive to see the reality to which such language is pointing.

We are not using the word "mystery" in the sense it is often used today. A mystery is not a riddle to be solved. We are closer to the New Testament usage of which G. S. Hendry says, "In the NT a mystery is a secret which has been, or is being, disclosed; but because it is a divine secret it remains mystery and does not become transparent to men."[2] We may, with many writers, contrast a mystery with a problem. A problem represents something unknown, and the appropriate reaction is to solve it. A problem haunts us until we find the solution, but once we know the solution the problem loses its interest. Nothing is more boring than a puzzle book after we have solved the puzzles. A problem or an unknown is something that is, at least in principle, knowable, even when we are unable at the moment to obtain further knowledge.

One is tempted to contrast a mystery with a problem by saying that a mystery is not unknown but unknowable. This is justifiable in that a man confronted with mystery is aware that he stands before that which his understanding can never encompass. But such a distinction misses the point, for the essence of a mystery is not a matter of knowledge or lack of knowledge. As our knowledge increases, the unknown diminishes; but it is not the case that, as knowledge increases, the mystery vanishes. On the contrary, mystery is inclined to increase. In the Bible the mystery of God is increased by his revelation of himself. As men's knowledge of God grows, their sense of the mystery of God increases. The principal mark of a mystery is not that it fills us with a sense of ignorance; on the contrary it fills us with awe, wonder, and reverence which quite frequently increase as knowledge grows. The man who knows all the biological causes and developments in the birth of a child may feel more keenly a sense of mystery as he gazes upon his firstborn than he would if he were ignorant of the biological factors.

It is not surprising to find that the sense of mystery is frequently experienced by the scientist. For example, Jean Henri Fabre, the entomologist, after studying the cross-pollination of flowers by insects, was filled with an overwhelming awe and said, "Before these mysteries of life, reason bows and abandons itself to adoration of the Author of these miracles."[3] It is obvious that this sense of mystery was not caused by his lack of knowledge but precisely by the increase of knowledge. It is interesting that, although he had discovered the scientific laws involved, he referred to them as "miracles." Here perhaps is the real meaning of miracle. A miracle is an event with the power to create the sense of wonder, awe, and reverence. Jesus was reluctant to perform miracles before a crowd that was seeking only cheap sensationalism and a good story to tell the folks back home. The miracle is truly a miracle only for him who is inspired by it to a sense of mystery. But an event that moves a man to see mystery is, in the truest sense, a miracle even though the natural laws involved are known to him.

To sum up the distinction between the unknown and a mystery, we may say that a man faced with the unknown has the sense of being ignorant. But the man faced with mystery is not properly described as ignorant. He is aware of being humbled and awe-inspired. He becomes aware of his finiteness. This is why mystery leads to worship. We cannot worship that of which we are simply ignorant. We may fear the unknown, and we may even seek to propitiate it with various stratagems, but we can worship only when we are in the presence of that which reveals to us our finitude by revealing its own mystery.

One of the curses of modern life is that man's sense of mystery is likely to be starved. He is preoccupied with progress in overcoming the unknown because such progress supplies him with new gadgets. Modern man comes to take the world for granted. He has no vital contact with nature. Kant said that two things filled his heart with wonder—the moral law within and the starry heavens above. But modern man has come to think of all morals as relative, so that if the moral law within becomes unduly insistent, he goes to his psychiatrist to have his "guilt complex" removed. And he never sees the starry heavens because the bright lights of the city blot them out. The neon signs of the city may stir a man's heart, but they do not move him with mystery. On the contrary, they are apt to make him cry, "See what we men can do!" even if he personally has no ability to fix a faulty light switch.

As Paul Tillich says, our age has come to see nature simply as something to be controlled and manipulated. "The system of finite interrelations which we call the universe has become self-sufficient. It is calculable and manageable and can be improved from the point of view of man's needs and desires."[4] Thus modern man buys his food at the grocery without any contact with the wonders of growing life. The milk he drinks is delivered in a sanitary bottle, and he never faces the miracle whereby a cow turns grass and water into milk. When he takes a back-to-nature vacation he goes to a commercialized vacation land where nature has been manipulated to the advantage of a profitable tourist trade. When nature is seen exclusively as something to be controlled and manipulated, man is deprived of his sense of awe in the face of its wonders.

Without the experience of mystery the meaning of the word "God" is distorted. Without mystery God is thought of in terms of the supreme manipulator of the universe, or he is considered to be a hypothesis no longer necessary to explain the universe. The proofs of God have lost their persuasiveness, not because men today can see their logical flaws more clearly than before, but because men have lost the sense of mystery. Kant, who criticized the logic of the teleological argument, nevertheless insisted that he could not speak of the argument without reverence. But if a man can face the order of nature and say, "So what?", he will see nothing in the teleological argument but a mistaken attempt to form an unnecessary hypothesis. On the other hand, if he meets the world with a sense of wonder, he will be moved by the teleological argument even as he sees its logically unpersuasive form.

Without a sense of mystery man complains that, if there were a God, he should be more evident. God, if he existed, would be clearly verifiable. A typical exponent of this attitude is Bertrand Russell. Asked if there was anything that would cause him to believe in God, Russell replied that if there should come a voice from the sky predicting everything that was to happen in the next twenty-four hours, including some very improbable events, and if the predictions proved true, he would be inclined to accept the belief that some kind of superhuman intelligence existed.[5] It is of just such an attitude that Jesus said, "An evil and adulterous generation seeks for a sign but no sign shall be given to it" (Matt. 12:39). Such seeking is sin because it demands that God show himself on our terms instead of on his terms. It is the refusal to see God through the mystery of the commonplace, the normal, that which is despised and rejected by practical men bent on manipulating the universe. We are like the men of old who

> were all looking for a king
> to slay their foes and lift them high;
> Thou cam'st a little baby thing
> That made a woman cry.
>
> —GEORGE MACDONALD

Life's mystery is pointed up by the strange question "Why is there anything at all?" As J. J. C. Smart says this is a question that he very much wants to ask, and yet when he asks it, it puts his head into a whirl.[6] At first the question seems most proper. As we examine the universe it is obvious that everything in it might not have existed. We can imagine some past accident to the earth which would have meant that today none of us or our earth would exist. It is easy to carry the thought further. Our universe itself might not have existed. This is what it means to say that this is a finite or contingent universe. And so it seems proper to ask why there is something and not nothing. And yet the minute we ask our heads begin to whirl. What kind of answer do we expect? Science can, in principle if not in fact, answer the question of why our universe exists *as* it does today by tracing the series of causal events back through the ages. But of course this does not answer our question because such explanation presupposes the existence of something. Science, then, cannot satisfy our question.

The cosmological argument for God's existence is obviously intended to respond to this problem, and it takes us back to the "First Cause" to explain why there is something and not nothing. But this runs into a host of logical problems. It has to say that God exists of necessity, and the meaning of this is not clear. Again, can a "First Cause" be considered a "cause" at all? Causation is a concept that applies to the relation of events within the universe, but to ask what caused the universe is like asking for the time on the sun. As a result, most philosophers today throw out the relevance of this question. The best rational answer to it, they say, is "Why shouldn't something exist?" Rationally it is impossible to find anything wrong with this reply. At some point we have to begin with the plain fact that something is. For one man that point is the First Cause and he cannot ask or answer why there is a First Cause. Probably what it means to say that the First Cause exists necessarily is that we cannot say why it exists. But another man says that he will begin from the fact that the universe exists and that he cannot ask or answer why it exists. And so our question "Why is there something and not nothing?" is rationally dissolved. But it won't go away.

As Smart continues, we cannot say that the philosopher who brushes the question aside with the equally good question "Why shouldn't there be something?" is guilty of a lack of intelligence or acumen. But Smart says that he should feel that he must accuse such a philosopher of "a certain superficiality, a lack of seriousness, a lack of reverence for reality."[7] And here Smart puts his finger on the real issue. The question of why there is something and not nothing is not, logically speaking, a question at all. It does not formulate any problem about the unknown for which we could seek a solution by making something known. But it does express a sense of awe, wonder, and reverence before the mystery of existence. This question is not the beginning of philosophy or metaphysics, as Heidegger claims; it is, rather, the end of philosophizing: it is the beginning of worship.[8]

One of the weaknesses of analytical philosophy has been a tendency to ignore the reality of mystery.[9] In its determination to make language meaningful and clear-cut, analytical philosophy has cavalierly ignored the mystery of life. It limits language to a tame description of the mundane world, and what cannot be said clearly is dismissed from further consideration. It is deemed improper to strain and stretch language in the attempt to say what cannot be said clearly. But such positivist trends divorce us from reality, for reality comes with the experience of mystery. Even in an age like ours, when mystery is largely ignored, it comes back to haunt us. Analytical philosophy, however, does not need to ignore mystery. We have seen that analytical philosopher Smart can see its relevance. And it should not be forgotten that the greatest of the analysts, Wittgenstein, had a deep sense of the mystery of life. If linguistic analysis aims to analyze the languages of man as they are actually used, it must recognize that man does attempt to speak about mystery. That man universally experiences mystery is indicated by the universal practice of worship. Furthermore, where man experiences mystery he tries to express it in a great variety of ways, including ritual, myth, poetry, paradox, and song.

In Romans 1:19–20 Paul tells us: "For what can be known about God is plain to them, because God has shown it to them. Ever since the creation of the world his invisible nature, namely, his eternal power and deity, has been clearly perceived in the things that have been made." This passage has become a source of considerable debate between natural and kerygmatic theologians. But it is dubious if it is relevant to the question of natural theology. Paul is not referring to anything like cosmological or teleological arguments in this passage. It would seem that he does have in mind the sense of mystery which man, as man, faces before the given world. What is made manifest is God's "eternal power and deity." That is, it is the awe-inspiring, the mysterious transcendence of God to which the things that are witness. This interpretation is justified because the passage goes on to hold men responsible for the sin of changing "the glory of the immortal God for images resembling mortal man or birds or animals or reptiles" (Rom. 1:23). In other words, man, filled with a sense of transcendent mystery, gives his worship to finite things. This is the nature of idolatry. It worships that which is not worthy of worship, that which is not the source of awe, wonder, and reverence.

Man universally is aware of mystery. That is the witness to God that is found among all nations. The sense of mystery is no proof of God. It is compatible with many views of God, and even the atheist may be aware of the mystery of the universe. Mystery does not prove God's existence, but it helps us to understand the use of theological language. Such language wrestles with the task of expressing the mystery of life.

The concept of mystery is heightened when we look to the Judaeo-Christian revelation. As Barth says, in revelation "the boundary between God and man becomes really visible, of which the most radical sceptic and atheist cannot even dream, for all his doubts and negations."[10] As the Biblical revelation unfolds we perceive Luther's point that even in revelation God is the hidden God; the revealed God is mystery. In the presence of the world man was struck with the mystery of existence; he was moved to awe, reverence, and worship. But, as Paul says, man perverted this; he turned his worship to the forces of nature. He did not see that what possesses mystery is not nature but He who created nature. The Biblical God reveals himself as the Holy Transcendent One. It is to him alone that worship is due.

Theological language points to the realm of mystery. The theologian who stands in the Judaeo-Christian tradition is trying to point to the mystery that transcends the created universe. A bystander might comment that this will be a good trick if you can do it. The theologian is armed with words, and it is his task to say the unsayable. Wittgenstein said that whereof one cannot speak one must be silent. E. P. Ramsey adds, "What we can't say we can't say, and we can't whistle it either."[11] But man is the communicating animal, and when he has an experience he feels called to communicate it. And, despite what Ramsey says, he can sometimes "whistle" what he cannot say. In music, art, poetry, drama, and particularly in the liturgy of worship he does communicate what he cannot say.

The proper language of mystery is the language of worship. The worshiping congregation sings, "We praise thee, we bless thee, we worship thee, we glorify thee, we give thanks to thee for thy great glory, O Lord God, heavenly king, God the Father Almighty." As the outsider listens he may suppose that the congregation is paying metaphysical compliments to the Deity. He may even conclude that this is being done to flatter God in order to win his benefits. No Christian would deny that there is always a danger that worship will become a subtle means of "lobbying for favors in the Courts of the Almighty." But when that happens worship has ceased to be worship. True worship is neither metaphysical compliment nor flattery; it is a response to, and an expression of, the mystery of God. The language of worship is not a means to an end; it is an end in itself.

The academic discipline known as theology is not the primary language of mystery. Therefore several writers have distinguished between "theological" and "religious" statements. For example, John Hutchison argues that religious statements are statements "in" religion and theological statements are "about" religion.[12] The function of theological statements is to study comprehensively and critically the religious statements.

There is value in recognizing that there is a different function between the language of "religion," in which God is addressed and worshiped, and the language of "theology," in which one attempts to understand the language of religion.

This corresponds roughly to the differing functions of the service of worship and the church school in the parish. Suspended somewhere between these are the creeds which may be used in worship but which are also attempts to understand the language of religion. However, it is dangerous to overemphasize these differences. In practice they are not sharply divided, and it is certain that they do not form different language games. Worship and technical theology belong to one language game just as passing and kicking are distinct functions but both a part of the game of football.

Technical theology does not have any independent material with which to work; its subject matter arises from the worshiping community. The work of the professional, or academic, theologian is simply an extension of the questions and answers that arise wherever Christian people try to understand their faith. Hutchison argues that theology is marked by the rise of "highly abstract and technical terms" and by "professional students of the subject matter."[13] This is true, but either the technical jargon of the professionals is translatable into the language of the worshiping comunity or it is a private game played by an esoteric group. At best, the professional theologian is a servant of the worshiping congregation; at worst, he is a parasite on it. The language of the professional ceases to be theological if he forgets that he speaks of the Mysterious Source of wonder and awe worshiped in the community of faith.

All theology, technical or otherwise, the Christian believes is possible only because God, the Mystery, has revealed himself. Barth puts it: "We could not utter one wretched syllable about the nature of the Word of God, if the Word of God had not been spoken to us as God's Word."[14] This is a point that will be explored more fully in the following chapters. But here it is important to see that, as Barth also reminds us, there needs to be a theological warning against theology. That is, theology must beware lest it create a graven image of words. Hywel D. Lewis points out that many religious apologists miss the point because they fail to take sufficient account of the radical difference between the idea of God and other notions that we have.[15] Unless theology is closely related to worship, it will always miss the point that the One of whom it speaks is mysteriously transcendent.

God reveals himself, the Christian believes, through concrete historical events, but the "hiddenness" of revelation means that it is always possible to interpret these events as other than a Word from God. The history of Israel may be interpreted as "Saving history" or as simply a part of ancient history. Jesus Christ may be seen as the Son of God or as a man who is judged to be either great or mad. The Church may be interpreted as the Body of Christ or as another sociological institution. The Bible may be seen as God's revelation or as an interesting ancient book of history, morals, and religion.

But not only is it possible to see these events as other than revelation, none of them can be simply identified with the transcendent God. When the Israelite people were prone to suppose that they could be identified with God, they were rudely reminded that judgment begins with the household of God (I Pet. 4:17). Although Israel was the chosen people, Israel's acts were never simply the acts of God. God stood in judgment over them. Although Jesus made claims for himself that made his revealing function clear (e.g., Matt. 10:32, 16:13–28), he could nonetheless ask why men inquired of him what was good when there is only one that is good, God. (Matt. 19:16, 17). Although Paul called the Church the Body of Christ (I Cor. 12:27), in the same letter he could force the Church to face its sinfulness in a radical manner (I Cor. 1:11–14, 5:1—6:11). Although Christians hold to the Bible as the supreme book of God's revelation, they have had to learn painfully that it is not itself divine.

God's revelation comes in forms that are, in one sense, inappropriate to the revelation. The transcendent and mysterious God appears speaking through finite things of the world. In a deeper sense, however, the means are appropriate, for only as such could they be revelation to finite man. But this does mean, as Paul puts it, that "we have this treasure in earthen vessels" (II Cor. 4:7). Nonetheless, this revelation through an earthly veil is not some second-rate revelation which can be superseded. Barth says, "Were God to speak to us in a non-worldly way, He would not speak to us at all."[16] We cannot overcome this veiled worldiness in any mystic vision.

Because God was hidden as well as revealed in Christ, it was possible for many to see, hear, and know about Jesus without knowing revelation. Today it is possible to read the New Testament and still not hear the Word of God speaking through Christ. Thus the first disciples knew and loved Christ well enough to follow him, but until Peter's confession they did not recognize him as the Christ. When Peter made his confession Jesus told him that "flesh and blood" had not revealed this to him, but that this was the work of God (Matt. 16:17). Luther put it in his exposition of the Holy Spirit in his Small Catechism: "I believe that by my own reason or strength I cannot believe in Jesus Christ, My Lord, or come to him. But the Holy Spirit has called me through the Gospel, enlightened me with his gifts, and sanctified and preserved me in true faith, just as he calls, gathers, enlightens, and sanctifies the whole Christian church on earth and preserves it in union with Jesus Christ in the one true faith."[17] Here is convictional language that points to the evidence itself. The Christian knows that God was in Christ reconciling the world because the Holy Spirit opens his ears to hear the mysterious significance of God's hidden work in Christ.

In the light of this brief summary in which we have seen that the transcendent God has revealed himself through finite means, it is clear that theological language will have a unique quality. It is no argument against theological language to show that it differs from our language about things. If it did not, it would not be language about God but language about another thing among the world of things. When we speak about the One who is mysteriously transcendent, it should not be strange to the analytical philosopher that we have to play a different language game. It was Wittgenstein who alerted us to look for differing shades of meaning when a word is used in differing contexts.

No doubt it is annoying to the philosopher when he hears

the theologian put forth an analogy to express the nature of God and then start "eroding" the analogy with a host of qualifications. But if the linguistic analyst abides by his own principles and analyzes language as it is actually used, he must see that this procedure is necessary to theology. How else can we speak about the transcendent Mystery except by using words that point toward it and then, reminding ourselves of their finite character, try to show where they fail to point. Perhaps we will erode the analogy so much that it will no longer point anywhere, and then theology has failed. But the process of taking away from our analogies is made necessary by the fact that we have to point with space-time terminology to that which transcends space and time. When you carry heavenly treasures in earthen vessels you ought to apologize for it.

Ian Ramsey says that religious language will be characterized by "oddness" and "logical impropriety."[18] His point is that, taking words from common speech, it uses them for an uncommon purpose. He finds similar oddness in poetry and certain scientific theories. Oddness is used to cause the hearer to see that which otherwise would have been missed. When the oddness accomplishes its purpose there is an opening of the eyes, a sense of "Aha, I get it!" or, as Ramsey likes to put it, "The penny drops, the light dawns."

The "logical oddness" of theological language appears when, on the basis of the conviction that God has revealed himself, we try to express his revelation. There are certain human relationships that bear an analogy to what we have to say. God's love is revealed to be like that of a father. But it is apparent that God is not in a literal sense our father, he is not the male parent of anybody. So we have to put in the qualifying term—he is a "heavenly" father. The adjective "heavenly" is the warning that "father" is being used in a logically odd way. It is significant that, although Jesus and the Jews before him called God father, they firmly rejected any concept of divine-human sexual relations such as were common in Greek mythology.

Because the language pictures used to point to God have

"oddness," it is necessary to use more than one picture. Jesus referred to God as the king whose kingdom was to come. There are aspects of God, as revealed to us, that are better expressed in terms of king and subject than in terms of father and son. But it won't do to conclude from this that, since God is both our father and a king, therefore we are princes. That would ignore the logical "oddity" of the expressions. And other metaphors and analogies are used. God is a judge, a shepherd, a rock of ages, a mighty fortress, a spirit, and so on. No one of these analogies or metaphors can be taken by itself and be allowed to stand. If any could be taken as a defining description of God, we would not be speaking of the transcendent; the mystery would be gone. The treasure cannot be carried in just one earthen vessel; it needs many.

But we are not free to choose analogies and metaphors at random. Each of these is in a way appropriate. God's revelation in Christ makes it clear that "fatherhood" is a most appropriate analogue. It points in a direction, and it communicates understanding. But it does not leave us free to deduce the full nature of God from the relations of earthly fathers to their children. On the contrary, the revealing of the Fatherhood of God transformed the concept of human fatherhood. One would not learn about God from watching the Roman father who practiced infanticide.

It may seem that we are caught in a vicious circle. We speak with analogies, and the analogies are all inadequate, all can mislead. However, as Wittgenstein has pointed out, that is always true of analogies, and it is never possible to draw a sharp line to denote where the misleading begins or ends. But he also goes on to emphasize that, nonetheless, analogies can be "extremely useful."[19] Too often we allow ourselves to fall into the trap of supposing that if we do not have complete knowledge of something, we have no knowledge at all. The theological "warning against theology" reminds us that we shall never lay bare the knowledge of God as a biologist can lay bare the inner parts of a dissected frog. (But even then the biologist cannot claim to know everything about the frog.) We need to say, "I know, help thou my ignorance."

From all of this it is obvious that theological language may find itself in paradox. We introduce this term with caution, for it is too easy, when caught in a contradiction, to look profound and to pontificate, "It is a paradox." But one cannot deny that there is something paradoxical about the whole theological enterprise. Kierkegaard saw this when he said, "The supreme paradox of all thought is the attempt to discover something that thought cannot think."[20] Theological paradox is legitimate when it is used to remind us that we are dealing with mystery. The great insight of Kierkegaard was to see that theological paradox is the point where our understanding must fail and we can do no more than point beyond it to the mystery that cannot be comprehended. The recognition of paradox and its use need not be an irrational act; it can be a means of pointing to mystery.

The philosopher is often maddened by the theologian who seems to retreat from every logical defeat into the fortress of mystery. But if the philosopher really wants to see the use of theological language, he must quiet his impatience long enough to understand. When he does, he may find that the theologian is engaged in sloppy thinking, which he hides by facile reference to paradox or mystery. And where there is a problem the philosopher must keep prodding the theologian to solve it and not to quit prematurely. But the philosopher, in all fairness, must see that theology, by its very nature, is pointing to mystery, and where that is the case it is pointless to complain because the theologian refuses to handle mystery as though it were a problem.

If we become intoxicated with the eroded analogies and paradoxes of theological language, we can reject the whole theological enterprise as the result of a series of language mistakes. But if, like a good linguistic analyst, we ask what is the use of this language, if we look to the community from which this language comes and the experience of mystery to which it is attempting to do justice, then its meaningfulness becomes apparent. Actually Ramsey's concept of the "logical oddness" of theological language is misleading. From the point of view of the man outside it may be logically odd. But many of science's statements, such as that the universe is finite but unbounded, are logically odd to the nonscientist. But within the community where the game is played the logic is not "odd" at all; it is necessary.

In the last chapter we argued that theological language is rooted in the community of faith. The paradigm case for all theological words is that community's use of these words. In the deepest sense the meaning of theological language cannot be understood until we have joined in the experience of worship. We cannot understand theological language unless we see that it is rooted in mystery, which motivates the response of worship. Quite literally, the man who has not worshiped cannot know what theological language is about, just as the man who has never experienced a sense of duty cannot know what ethical language is about. This means that theology is possible only when it begins in worship and moves toward its end and goal in worship. Although theology deals with problems, it is never primarily a problem-solving venture: it is the servant of the worshiping community. When theology forgets this it ends in a futile maze of verbiage.

Today it has become popular to say that theology is "irrelevant" and "meaningless" to modern man. We are called to reconstruct the language of theology, to demythologize it, and in various ways to make it relevant to the modern world. We have already emphasized that there are problems for theological language in the contemporary age. Bonhoeffer's letters from prison are hailed as the trumpet call to a new language that will leave "religion" behind and speak to a world that has "come of age." But Bonhoeffer made a point that is often overlooked by his enthusiastic followers. He saw that a new language could be born only out of prayer and service to our fellow men.[21] It was here that Bonhoeffer himself found strength and a new life in prison.[22] It is no accident that today, though college students widely express the modern critique of theological language, worship services and the Lord's Supper win a response from them. This indicates that the first vital step to understanding the nature of theological language is being made in worship.

We have argued that the Church is a community of faith called into being by the power of the mystery of God. This illuminates the convictional framework of the Christian faith. There is no argument to demonstrate that man's experience of mystery is significant or important, or that it is a knowledge of a reality. Like the experience of the material world or the experience of ethical obligation, the experience of mystery has its own power to convict man. The man so convicted can only witness to his convictor; he can invite the other to come "and live with him" in confidence that the other will be convicted also. But now we can see that the invitation for the other to come "and live with him" is basically an invitation to come "and worship with him."

NOTES

[1] J. A. T. Robinson, *op. cit.*, pp. 45–46.

[2] See A. Richardson, *A Theological Word Book of the Bible,* (New York: Macmillan Company, 1951), p. 156.

[3] Quoted by C. A. Coulson, *Science and Christian Belief* (Chapel Hill: University of North Carolina Press, 1955), p. 86.

[4] P. Tillich, *Theology of Culture* (New York: Oxford University Press, 1959), p. 43.

[5] See L. Rosten (ed.), *A Guide to the Religions of America* (New York: Simon and Schuster, 1955), p. 157.

[6] See A. Flew and A. MacIntyre (eds.), *New Essays in Philosophical Theology,* pp. 18 ff.

[7] *Ibid.,* p. 19.

[8] M. Heidegger, *An Introduction to Metaphysics,* transl. by R. Manheim (Garden City: Doubleday & Co., 1961), p. 14.

[9] For example see M. B. Foster, *Mystery and Philosophy* (London: SCM Press, 1957), chap. 1.

[10] K. Barth, *Church Dogmatics,* I.2., transl. by G. T. Thomson and H. Knight (New York: Charles Scribner's Sons, 1956), p. 29.

[11] Quoted by A. J. Ayer, in Ayer *et al., The Revolution in Philosophy,* p. 75.

[12] J. Hutchison, *Language and Faith* (Philadelphia: Westminster Press, 1963), p. 227.

[13] *Ibid.,* p. 240.

[14] K. Barth; *Church Dogmatics,* I.1, p. 187.

[15] See Ian Ramsey (ed.), *Prospect for Metaphysics* (London: George Allen & Unwin, 1961), p. 206.

[16] K. Barth, *Church Dogmatics,* I.1, p. 192.

[17] See T. G. Tappert (ed.), *The Book of Concord* (Philadelphia: Muhlenberg Press, 1959), p. 345.

[18] I. T. Ramsey, *Religious Language* (London: SCM Press, 1957), pp. 37–38.

[19] L. Wittgenstein, *The Blue and Brown Books,* p. 28.

[20] S. Kierkegaard, *Philosophical Fragments,* transl. by D. F. Swenson (Princeton: Princeton University Press, 1936), p. 29.

[21] D. Bonhoeffer, *Prisoner for God,* pp. 140–141.

[22] *Ibid.,* pp. 65–71, 77, 89.

8

THE PERSONAL LANGUAGE GAME

Professional theologians seem always to be in danger of falling into one of two errors. Sometimes, forgetting the mystery of God, they set out confidently to describe God within their systems. Seeing the pretentious error of this, other theologians lose their nerve and assume that nothing can be said about God. In Christian faith a way can be found between these errors. Because Christian faith recognizes the transcendence of God, it can never suppose that its words capture the mystery of God. But, because it believes that God has revealed himself, it is convinced that it has a base of knowledge from which it can speak. In the preceding chapter our emphasis was upon the mystery of God. In this and the next chapter our emphasis will be upon God as he makes himself known. But the two emphases must never be separated.

It is the conviction of Christians that God has revealed himself to man through the events of Israel's history and through Jesus Christ. Theological language attempts to communicate this revelation. We saw that analytical philosophy criticizes the analogical method of speaking about God because, until we have nonanalogical knowledge, we cannot even know where there is an analogy.[1] Thus, if we know nothing about God, analogy cannot be a means of coming to knowledge about him. It is our thesis, however, that God in his revelation gives knowledge of himself. On the basis of this knowledge it is apparent that certain analogies are appropriate in speaking about God.

When we examine the Bible we find that many analogies and metaphors are used when referring to God. But both Testaments return continually to language drawn from personal relations. Not only does the Bible speak of God as king and father, but it portrays God as acting, speaking, willing, loving, judging, and so on. To grasp the significance of this way of speaking of God we need, first, to see that among man's language games is that of personal relations. Like other games, this language has its own logic and uses. Secondly, we need to see that the revelation of God through the Scripture makes it plain that, although no human language game can be translated into language about God, the language game that points with the least obscurity to God is that of personal language. This is rooted in the fact that God offers to man a personal relationship with himself. While there is little analogy between our knowledge of things and our knowledge of God, there is a real analogy between our knowledge of persons and our knowledge of God. Wittgenstein says that every language game overlaps with some other game. Our thesis is that theological language has most in common with personal language.

Of course, in speaking about the personal nature of God we do not forget the mystery of God. God is not a glorified old man up in heaven. Even when using its most anthropomorphic language about God, the Bible never forgets his awe-full majesty (for example, see Exod. 19:3–25). Some thinkers prefer to call God "suprapersonal." This is useful to remind us that created personality is an inadequate expression of God's mystery. But, in saying that God is suprapersonal we must not suppose that we have said anything positive about God. He is no doubt more than what we know as personal, but we cannot know what the "more" is. Barth seems to be on firmer ground when he says that the question is not "Is God a person" but "Are we?"[2] That is, as God reveals his person he brings a judgment on our failure to become true persons.

Through the history of theology there always have been objections to using personal language to refer to God. In our time this objection has been expressed most forcefully by Paul Tillich. He objects to speaking of God as *a person*. This concept, he alleges, originated only in the nineteenth century. In classical theology, he says, the term "person" was applied to the hypostases of the Trinity but not to God himself. He grants that it is fundamental to think of God as personal because man cannot be ultimately concerned with anything less than the personal. But because popular theism is based on the personal view of God, Tillich claims that atheism is correct over against it. He concludes, " 'Personal God' is a confusing symbol."[3]

In answer to Tillich we would first question his historical statement. Is it true that the concept of God as a person did not appear before the nineteenth century? Luther, Calvin, Augustine, Wesley, and most other great theologians spoke of God in a fashion that makes it legitimate to conclude that they were thinking of God as a person. Samuel Laeuchli has made a convincing case that the second century theologian Irenaeus speaks and thinks of God in terms that can only be called personal.[4] It is true that one tradition of Trinitarian interpretation, that of the Cappadocian Fathers, used the concept of person in something like its contemporary meaning, to apply only to the members of the Trinity. But the Western tradition, following Augustine, has recognized that personality is to be applied to God inasmuch as man is created in the image of the Trinity and not in the image of one member of the Trinity.[5] Tillich's claim that atheism is correct against popular theism is ambiguous. If by popular theism Tillich means some of the popular ideas of the "man upstairs," we would agree. We must not forget the element of mystery. But this salutary warning does not exclude the possibility of a more adequate understanding of God's person.

Some theologians would say that we may think of God as "personal" but not as "a person." But this is not helpful. Anything "personal" that does not exist in a person is rather like the smile of the Cheshire cat after the cat has gone. Certainly we can show that the concept of God as a person is a most appropriate way of speaking about God as he is revealed in the Bible. A person possesses certain character traits, and the Biblical God is so presented. He is describable by traits such as loving, merciful, trustworthy, righteous, and he is not describable by terms such as vindictive and unjust. He is capable of decision and action, which are marks of an individual. As Cyril Richardson puts it, "It is by His *particularity* that God is the living God."[6] When the Christian witnesses to his experience of the Biblical God he speaks about a person-to-person encounter, the relation of an "I" to a "thou." Personal relationships are meaningful only between individuals. Without doubt God is more than what we mean by "a person," but the point is that the only God we know comes to us as a person.

Furthermore, it is obvious that when men try to find a better way to refer to God than as a person they defeat their purpose. They wish to express God in terms higher than personality, but what they say describes God in less than personal terms. As Tillich himself concedes, a man could not be in communication with God if "he were only 'ultimate being.'"[7] And, we must ask, is this not because "ultimate being" is a lesser concept than personality? Aristotle wanted to refer to God as First Cause, but the concept of a cause lacks many attributes of the person. Einstein, in keeping with the practice of many scientists, preferred to think of God as "rational cosmic intelligence," but this is to make God the great computer in the skies. It takes only one aspect of a person—his mind—and makes that the sole feature of God.

All such attempts to think of God as more than personal result in the predicament that Niebuhr finds in idealist attempts to think of God as "the Absolute." "This philosophy involves itself in an absurdity in the effort to escape an absurdity; it defines God in terms of all kinds of 'absolutes'; but its God lacks the simple majesty of the freedom which man undoubtedly has."[8] That is, the attempt to describe God in more than personal terms ends up by treating him as less than personal.

Since God has revealed that the key to speaking about him lies in the realm of personal language, the theologian needs to investigate the nature of personal language. In our day we have been conditioned to suppose that scientific knowledge is the perfect model for all forms of knowledge. In science, we believe, there is the closest thing to certainty that man can have, for here the great conquests in the realm of knowledge have been made. Logical positivism was a philosophical expression of a mood that is widespread in our time, the mood which assumes that if anything is not scientific knowledge, it cannot be knowledge at all. This is the hidden premise in most attacks on theological language that still come from analytical philosophers. Consequently theology has been tempted to formulate its beliefs in terms of an analogy with the findings of science. But to do so is to assume, however subtly, that God is to be thought about as a thing. Furthermore, it is to overlook the fact that, although science has been dramatic in its results, there always has been another form of knowledge that is crucial for life—the knowledge of persons. Even the purest of scientists does not try to know his wife as a "specimen" or as a complex differential equation. Or perhaps we should say, if he does, his marriage will be a tragedy.

In recent years a number of philosophers in the analytical school have been engaged with the problem of knowledge of other minds. It is strange that earlier philosophy did not spend more time on this fascinating subject, for it is full of philosophical complexities. But most analytical philosophers have failed to attain depth because they have forgotten that "mind" is only a part of a person. Thus Gilbert Ryle, in his helpful book *The Concept of Mind,* argues persuasively that I understand another person's mind when I understand what he does. Understanding is a part of knowing how, he tells us, so that when I know how to do what the other person is doing I understand his mind. We understand the mind of Euclid when we can do his geometry.[9] All this may be true, but it is not the way we get to know Euclid as a person. We may understand the whole of Euclidean geometry and still have little idea of what kind of person Euclid was.

In fact, in his discussion Ryle consistently seems to miss an ambiguity in the common question "Wouldn't you like to know what goes on in his mind?" This question may mean quite literally "How does his *mind* work?", in which case

Ryle seems correct when he answers, "Overt intelligent performances are not clues to the workings of minds; they are those workings."[10] But in most cases in which this question arises the questioner would not feel that Ryle had answered him, for the question is normally asked by people who want to know, "What kind of *person* is he?" That is, they are not interested only in the logical workings of his mind, they also want to know about his character, his dreams, hopes, fears, ambitions, and so on. They want to know whether the self that he reveals is his real self or a mask worn for a variety of purposes. Knowing persons means much more, as we shall try to show, than knowing how they play chess, to use one of Ryle's favorite illustrations. We want to know the motivations for their decisions, the dominating commitments of their lives. We want to know what makes them a person and not a walking and talking computer.

Later analytical philosophy approaches personal language. Thus Stuart Hampshire finds the essence of such language in the fact that the person is an "agent" who performs acts with purposes and intentions.[11] However, we need to listen to existentialist philosophers in addition to the linguistic analysts at this point. The nature of personal language has been illuminated also by novelists, psychotherapists, and theologians.

We have said that the average person who asks, "What is going on in his mind?" is probably looking for something more than what Ryle defines as mind. Is it possible to say what this "more" is? It is unlikely that we can produce any simple definition of this "more," but perhaps a series of illustrations will indicate what we are referring to.

To begin with, each person is aware of being a self. We become conscious of this through contact with our environment. What first distinguishes our environment from our selves is probably the fact that it fails to act continuously according to our wishes. As a part of this environment we meet other persons, and a clash of our wills with their wills stimulates self-consciousness.

In the second place, one comes to know his self as a self because of the need to make decisions. At the dawn of thought the baby finds that he does not have to wait passively for his environment to satisfy his wishes. He can act upon it. He begins to distinguish between what happens to him and what he does. In Hampshire's terms, he comes to know himself as an "agent."[12] But when we know ourselves as agents, the initiators of events, we also realize that we have to make decisions as to which acts we should perform. Thus, through meeting an environment and through making decisions we become aware of being a self.

As we begin to speak about our "self" we note that language begins to get "odd." When I speak of knowing my self I am playing a different language game from the games used when I say that I know a book or a mathematical theorem. For the "self" that I know and the "I" that knows are not two entities but one. As Langmead Casserley puts it, " 'I know I,' although deporably bad syntax, would express the truth about self-consciousness more accurately."[13] The normal subject-object division that occurs in our language about things is absent when we are speaking about our selves or, if used, must be recognized as having a different logic.

In becoming aware of being a self we are aware of having various sensations. We see colors, feel pains, know hunger, and so on. As one reads the analytical philosophy's discussion of knowing other minds it often seems that the most important part of knowing other minds is to know about such sensations. But one of our debts to existentialism is that it has demonstrated that self-consciousness involves much more than sensations. As we become aware of being agents who make decisions we know that behind acts lie motives and purposes. Some of the motives we find good and some less good. An important element in decision lies in choosing between motives that we find desirable and motives that we evaluate as more worthy. Thus decision involves varying degrees of anxiety and passion. As life is lived we find that we are committed to certain basic patterns, certain things have gripped us as being ultimately worthwhile, we have developed a "character."

The self is often a battleground of various forces. Sometimes the self feels lost among these and has to ask, "Who am I?" This is no easy question. Early in life the self is the child of the parents, the follower, more or less willingly, of their will. At some point there is rebellion from parental authority, but this normally results in capitulating to the authority of some other person or group. Existentialist philosophy has wrestled with the problem of how man can live "authentically." That is, so long as the self is simply a pawn pushed by external forces it lives inauthentically. To become authentic the self must make its own decisions. We do not need to accept some of the existentialist's almost paranoid fear of other persons to recognize that there is a world of difference between two men performing similar actions when one is acting authentically and the other is not. In the last analysis the self must answer the question, "Who am I?" by making decisions and commitments.

As we come to know our selves we become aware that we have an element of choice as to how we reveal our selves to others. At an early date we learn to wear a mask. When bored we learn not to show it. We seethe with anger but hide it. We hate a man but pretend to like him. We rationalize our motives to make them appear more worthy and in the process often fool ourselves. At times we realize, with pleasure or pain, that we have associated with someone for a long time and have given him little idea of who we really are. Our awareness that we do not always reveal our selves truly to others through our acts and words gives rise to the haunting question, "I wonder what is going on in his mind?" That is, we want to know whether the other person is truly revealing his self or whether he is wearing a mask. We wonder whether we really know other people, and, as novelists know, this question is full of dramatic appeal. The question is not a "philosophical" one that arises when the engine of thought is idling. It comes from the daily life of every man.

Considerations of this kind are glossed over by all too many philosophical discussions of "other minds." For example, logical positivism, having limited meaningful statements to those that are empirically verifiable or true a priori, had to claim that meaningful statements about other persons are always translatable into statements about the observable physical behavior of the other person. As Rudolf Carnap puts it, "*All sentences of psychology describe physical occurrences, namely, the physical behavior of humans and other animals.*"[14] We may call this position "philosophical behaviorism."

Philosophical behaviorism, of course, cannot even raise the question of whether the self revealed by a man is his real self. Likewise, it can find no meaning in the distinction between authentic and inauthentic actions. The physical behavior of the man who gives to charity because public opinion has coerced him into the action and that of the man who gives from out of desire to help the less fortunate are identical. Yet in fact all men know that the difference between the two acts is of the utmost importance.

Yet even within the logical-positivist scheme philosophical behaviorism has difficulties. References to the self of others that go beyond reference to physical behavior are not simply unverifiable and hence meaningless according to the logical-positivist system. On the contrary, they are often, if not always, verifiable by one person. In baseball the umpire is empowered to discipline a pitcher who throws a ball at the batter if it is done "intentionally." Everyone knows that there is a world of difference between intentionally throwing a ball at a batter's head and doing the same thing by accident. And yet seldom is there a physically observable difference between the two events. Therefore umpires seldom invoke the rule. But even when they do not, the batter may shout in anger, "You did that on purpose." When he does the crowd definitely knows what he means. Furthermore, everyone knows that although the statement is not verifiable by the batter, the umpire, or the crowd, it is completely verifiable by one person —the pitcher.

Here is a situation that strains the verification theory of logical positivism. If by definition we say that there is no "verification" when something is verifiable by only one, then we can say that statements about premeditation and intention are "emotive." But what reason is there for so changing the normal meaning of the words? When we say, "You know you did that on purpose," we are not speaking "metaphysically"; we are affirming that, in the normal sense of the words, the other person can *know*.

Similar situations are found in more crucial personal relations. A wife asks her husband, "Do you really love me?" If the husband accepts the behaviorist position, he might answer, "Why do you ask? You see my love, I support you, I give you a good home and fine clothes, I kiss you when I go to work, I take you out to dinner regularly, I have sexual intercourse with you, and I say that I love you. What more do you want?" It is a noted fact, however, that this does not answer the question. All these acts could be motivated by something quite other than love. When a person asks such a question, and it is a universal question in life, no answer in terms of behaviorism will still the hunger from which it arises. This is a question about the self of the other, and it cannot be translated totally into physical actions.

In discussing logical positivism we argued that it was a reasonable description of scientific meaning. We can agree that philosophical behaviorism does describe all that is scientifically discernible about the self. What we do affirm is that we seek and often attain a knowledge of other persons which is not a scientific knowledge and which is neither verifiable nor falsifiable within the language game of science. But it is, nonetheless, verifiable within its own game.

The theory that all statements about another self can be translated into actions about his bodily activity is not plausible. But there is a half-truth in it. Our knowledge of other persons comes primarily, and perhaps exclusively, through their bodily actions. At present we are not in a position to deny that there are forms of mental telepathy. But even if we do believe that we have received knowledge through such means, we must seek to verify it through the bodily actions of the other person, including speech. What behaviorism misses is that our concern is not with knowing the bodily acts as such but with knowing the self who is expressing himself through the actions. Words and acts are the means through which a self makes itself known to others.

We are not advocating the view that man consists of a soul (or mind) and a body with the soul "using" the body. Ryle has aptly called this the theory of the "Ghost in the Machine," and no Christian ought to object to the ridicule that Ryle heaps upon it.[15] The Biblical view of man knows nothing of a body-soul dichotomy; it sees man as a unity. When we say that the physical actions are an expression of man's self we are not claiming some kind of ghostly existence for the self within the body. We are saying that we express through physical actions something more than physical actions.

Something of what we are trying to say is expressed by Wittgenstein when he says, "What is left over if I subtract the fact that my arm goes up from the fact that I raise my arm?"[16] Wittgenstein is not trying to argue for some ghost within the body that somehow causes the arm to rise, but he is making the obvious point that there is a real difference between "my arm goes up" and "I raise my arm." The self is not necessarily involved in the first statement, but in the second the self is pointed to as the agent acting in the moving arm. The second statement describes more than a physical action.

The point is even clearer when we turn to ethics. Most persons get the point when Paul says that if he gives away all that he has but has not love, it gains him nothing (I Cor. 13:3). That is, the physical act of giving to the poor cannot be judged good or bad until we know *why* it was done. The action in the physical world is an expression of the self not because the self is another thing hidden within the body but because the self, being an agent with the power of will and action, has a freedom of revealing or hiding its true nature. In other words, a part of being human is to have a private life.

We know other selves only through their bodily actions, including what they say. And yet, to know another person is to know more than the fact that he behaves in such and such a way; it is to know him as a self or an agent. We can express this fact by defining the acts by which a man reveals his self as the man's "word." Often the "word" takes the form of words, but sometimes it can be expressed only through actions.

In Albert Camus's novel *The Plague* a man who had lived in the city through the plague found it impossible to tell others of the experience. Such a person spoke from out of the depths of long days of personal stress, passion, and pain. But what he said was said in the conventional terms of the masses and the marketplace; it could not describe the unique event that he had known. This is also the problem of speaking to a man in the midst of his tragedy. His tragedy is unique, and he is suffering it to the dregs. What we say are the typical words spoken in everyone's time of trouble. And so they sound trite and stereotyped; they are not an adequate "word" with which to express the self in this moment. In such situations the greatest comfort may come from one who says something common and trite but says it in a tone of voice that carries more meaning than the words. Or it may come from one who says nothing but who brings a gift, or who sits and weeps. In such situations it is literally correct to say that the actions *speak* louder than words. They speak because they communicate from self to self, they are a part of what we mean by the "word."

The term "word" is used also to remind us that if a person is to be known as a person, he must reveal his self through his acts and words. We can extract all of the knowledge we desire from a chemical or a rat in a maze or a corpse on a medical student's table, even though the objects in question do not cooperate in making themselves known. We do not expect any "word" from them. But we can never get to know a person this way. He must act to reveal his self. He may reveal his self unconsciously and we will learn something of him, but to know him in the fullest sense we must have his conscious desire to make his self known. This is a primary way in which knowledge of persons differs from knowledge of things. We depend on the person to reveal himself. If he refuses to cooperate, we can learn little; and if he consciously chooses to deceive us, we can only hope to outwit him. Knowledge of things never runs into this kind of complication.

We can use words or acts to give information to another

person. But when our words and acts become a "word" that reveals our self, it is not correct to say that we use our "word" to reveal our self. In the person-to-person relationship of revealing our self our "word" is our self. This is why we can say of a man that, even though his words may be true, he is living a lie. That is, he is not the "word" that he speaks. This is the point that Kierkegaard saw. In science we can speak of true statements only, but in personal relations we speak of being the truth and thus of "true men."[17]

We can know another person only if he reveals his self, but there is another prerequisite to knowing another person. We must respond to the "word" that is spoken. We come to know things by simply observing them, and we do not have to give of ourselves to them. But, as Martin Buber taught us, in an I-thou relation there has to be response. We come to know most fully only those to whom we are prepared to reveal our selves. Confidence wins confidence. It is possible to know another self when he has revealed himself through his writings. But we have to make a response of sympathetic understanding. To know another we need empathy, the ability to put ourselves, to some degree, in the other's place. The completely self-centered person can never get to know someone else, for he cannot really come to feel with the other. He can neither make the revelation of his self to win revelation from the other, nor can he imagine himself into the other's position with empathy.

But we are all self-centered to some degree, and therefore we never get to know the other person fully. Always in our knowledge of the other there is some projection of ourselves. If we want to learn of John Smith and ask ten of his friends about him, we shall probably get ten different, and in some cases contradictory, pictures. This will be due in part to the fact that John has revealed differing aspects of his self to the different persons, but it will be due also to the fact that each person has projected something of himself onto his picture of John Smith. Knowing another person is always a two-way street. Knowing things requires intelligence, training, and diligence. But in knowing other persons these are not as important as is ethical character. Jesus said that the pure in heart would see God. It is not an unconnected fact that it is the pure in heart who see most truly their fellowmen.

One of the barriers to personal relations is that often we fail to reveal our self even to those to whom we sincerely desire to do so. A father sits down to agonize over the fact that his actions and words over the years have failed to become a "word" that expressed his true self to his child, so that today father and child do not know each other. After working with the same people for years a man pauses to reflect, "None of them knows the real me." A marriage is breaking up and the wife realizes that she never did manage to let her husband know who she was. There is something universal about the cry "No one understands me." We need to be understood by others, and this means far more than that we need others who can predict our actions. It means that we need those who can see our behavior as a "word" that we speak to reveal our self. Normally we blame others for not understanding us, but frequently we have failed to reveal our selves, and thus the relation of I to thou is stillborn.

On the other hand, despite the difficulties, most people are blessed with at least a few enduring personal relations in which they know and are known. In such relations people gladly reveal their selves and are rewarded by the answering revelation of the other. Such experiences prove that it is possible to know another person as a person, to see his behavior as a "word" that speaks from out of the full self and communicates with one who responds with his "word."

Such experiences are necessary to life. In a "Peanuts" cartoon Charlie Brown is asked what he will be when he grows up, and he answers, "Lonely." What is funny in such humor is difficult to analyze, for here is laid bare the basic tragedy of life—aloneness and estrangement from others. When Franz Kafka symbolizes such estrangement in his story "The Metamorphosis" we do not laugh, we tremble.

Knowledge of persons always depends upon trust. Although the wife needs to hear her husband tell her again and again that he loves her, the scientist does not need the same reassurance that hydrogen and oxygen are still uniting to form water.

But even when the husband replies that he does love his wife, the element of trust is not suspended. It never occurs to the scientist that oxygen may have been deceiving him all these years about its properties. But we can never have such certainty that a person has not masked his true self from us. Furthermore, any attempt to prove empirically another's trustworthiness will destroy the relationship in which we come to know the other as a self. If a husband hires a private detective to prove scientifically the faithfulness of his wife, the marriage is destroyed even if the detective reports her to be faithful.

Because personal relationships involve trust, we often say that love is blind. But more often it is the case that love sees what others have missed. Love sees, in part, because it pauses to listen to the "word" of the other as it is expressed in person-to-person relations. It also sees because it makes the revelation of the self that moves the other to make an answering revelation. Love thus comes to know another person as no behavioristic study or casual acquaintance could hope to do.

When we speak of knowing the self of another we find that we have to speak of trust, love, and the like. As a result our age is likely to object that this is poetry. It may have beauty, but it is not cognitively relevant, it is not knowledge. When we see the complications in knowing persons and the demands this knowing makes upon the knower, it is not surprising that some men have argued that only scientific knowledge is knowledge. The rules for scientific knowledge can be laid out neatly and clearly, and they cost little in terms of asking the knower to give of himself. And yet this theory, for all its neatness and clarity, is a patent absurdity. It arises from the mistake of supposing that the paradigm of knowing is our knowledge of the material world. Because the other person's "mind" is not located like a material object, we wonder how we can get to know it at all. But, argues John Macmurray, if we examine empirically the growth of knowledge, it is obvious that the child first comes to know other persons, particularly the mother. Only slowly does the child come to see that some entities in his environment are not persons but things. Primitive people, with their animistic world view, demonstrate that it was only after great effort that man developed the ability to recognize things as being inanimate.[18]

Macmurray concludes from this that there is no problem of how we know other persons, for here we learn what knowledge means. We know other persons because we are persons, and between persons there can be revelation and response, there can be communion. The real epistemic problem is how can we, who are persons, come to know things that are not personal? The precision of scientific knowledge lies in the fact that it is a reduced form of knowledge, a knowledge that gains its success because it aims at so little.[19]

Macmurray's point is well taken. The philosopher who calmly assumes that he knows the inanimate world and then, by analogy with this knowledge, asks how he can know other persons is a humorous figure. He reminds us of Kierkegaard's comic philosopher who built a beautiful castle of thought and then chose to live in the kennel. But today's philosophers are more comic than Kierkegaard's. They live in the castle but think that it is a kennel. That is, scientific or philosophical knowledge is valuable only because we first live in a community of persons whom we know, love, and admire. Within this community scientific knowledge plays a most important role, but it is the means and not the end. Who would want to be a scientist or a philosopher on a desert island where there was no one with whom to share one's discoveries? And yet the philosopher is sure that he knows things and wonders how he can know other minds. Perhaps there is something comical about the primitive man who thinks that there is a spirit in the tree, but he is not half so comical as the behaviorist who cannot see the self in his wife.

To know another person is to know a unique individual. This is why we argued that we may know Euclid's *mind* when we know how to do Euclidean geometry but that we do not get to know Euclid as a person in that fashion. All that Euclidean geometry tells us about Euclid is that he had certain intellectual capacities shared by millions through history. To know Euclid as a person, however, is to know him in his uniqueness. Of course, no individual is absolutely unique. Human beings share certain general patterns which provide a basis for understanding others. But each individual, due to his own particular history and to his unique decisions in living, becomes a unique person. In life we long to know and be known as unique persons.

Logicians are of little help when it comes to a question of knowing the unique. Wittgenstein argued that many philosophical problems arise from the philosopher's "contemptuous attitude towards the particular case."[20] Science cannot predict the exact dimensions of a single leaf before it buds. It can only predict in general that it will have the characteristics of an oak leaf and not those of a maple leaf. Although reality comes to us in the form of individuals, it is the aim of science to go from the individual to a universal law as quickly as possible. Although the scientist can predict generally what will happen with every repetition of an experiment, he cannot forecast in detail the results of any single experiment. Thus George Boas can say, "Reason stops short when confronted with individuals."[21]

In the physical sciences this inability to gain knowledge of the unique is not disturbing. It can only be called a "limitation" of science in a forced sense of the word "limitation," for we have no scientific interest in individual atoms, leaves, or cats. Science seeks the general principles that can be applied to all things in the class in question. If science did not so limit its concern, it could not be doing what science now does.

But when we turn to persons we are primarily concerned with the individual. A young man does not fall in love with a specimen of the class of females, aged twenty, good-looking, likable, socially adjusted, and so on. On the contrary, he falls in love with Mary Jones, and his love is directed precisely to those aspects of Mary that make her unique. Here is the distinction between love and lust. Lust seeks any female who meets certain minimum qualifications. But in love there is no one who can take the place of the unique person who is loved.

Milton Mayer brought out our point in a profound way.

Speaking of his late friend and agent George Bye, he said, "There are those of whom we say, when they die, that we shall not look upon their likes again. This is not what bothers me about George. What bothers me about George is that I shall not look upon *him* again."[22] That strikes home to anyone who has had a friend. If we only wished to replace George by someone with the same capacities, a battery of psychological tests could find someone to take George's place in the organization and to do his work. But it would not be George, and it would not replace him for his friends and loved ones.

To know persons we need a different methodology from that used in getting to know things. The ways of science will not gain the kind of knowledge that Milton Mayer had of his friend. Thus F. Waismann says of the theory that psychological statements can be reduced to complicated statements about the physical behavior of the person involved, "The whole thing rests on a naïveté—that there is one basic language (suitable for describing the behavior of rats) into which everything else must be translated . . . psychological statements belong to a stratum of their own, with a logic different from that of the language in which you say how a person looks, how he smiles, in short what he has in common with a rat."[23] What Waismann is saying, of course, is that knowledge of persons requires its own language game.

The words of personal language will not have the precision of the technical words of science, but they will be more expressive. Their denotations will be more vague, but their connotations will be richer. The poet has no place in scientific language, but in personal language he does have a place. Precisely because he plays fast and loose with the general meaning of words, he can often express the unique more adequately in poetry than in prose.

We see something of the logic of personal language if we examine how we try to report a person to a third person. As I think of a man I may try to describe him by saying that he is a middle-aged businessman. Immediately the hearer places him in a category with other middle-aged businessmen. If I add that he is a graduate of Yale, a Protestant, is honest, and his IQ is 125, the category gets smaller, but still the hearer will see only a member of a class. He will not see the unique individual. Some would say that when you have described all of the categories to which the man belongs you have said all that can be said about him. It is true that when we have described all of the categories to which a chemical belongs we have said about all that can be said about it. But man is not a chemical. Personal language will use this kind of description only as a background against which truly personal statements can be made.

To report on the self of the man in question we must change our tactics completely. We must start telling stories about him. We describe a situation and how he acted in it. We may have said that he is honest, and that put him into a category, but honesty is a vague term. If, however, we tell a story of what he did in a particularly tempting circumstance, you may say, "Oh, I see, he *really* is honest!" If we had a complete description of a man in the first kind of language, we would have placed him in a small category and know thousands of facts about him, but when we met him we would not likely say, "I feel that I already know you." But we do automatically say this when we meet someone about whom we have heard many anecdotes. Through the relating of "what he did when" we have seen the "word" by which he expresses his self. This is why certain institutions, in asking for a reference, request the telling of concrete incidents about the person.

P. F. Strawson says that when we are making a unique reference, "the context of utterance is of an importance which it is almost impossible to exaggerate."[24] Science tries to get statements completely free from particular references. The scientific equation is the model of scientific statement. It describes all situations in general and none in particular. But in personal language we must get away from the general and to the particular as soon as possible. Consequently the meaning of scientific statements does not change with the tone of voice, with who says it to whom, or where it is said. But the meaning of a personal statement is never complete until we know such facts about the situation in which it is said.

Not all events are of equal value in getting to know a person. We saw earlier that the wife who asks her husband if he loves her is not satisfied by a recital of his habitual support and habits. But if an unusual situation arises, the husband's actions may cause her to exclaim, "You really do love me!" In coming to know persons we need "special revelation." Certain acts form a "word" that reveal a person as others do not. If we are writing a biography of a person, our concern may be to catalogue the events of his life. The result will be dull. But if our aim is to point to the real person, we must carefully choose to relate those of his actions that form a "word" through which his true self is revealed. The four Gospels are a most unsatisfactory biography in the first sense. Their brevity is such that we get only a small fragment of the day-by-day doing of Jesus. But by the second standard they are perfect biographies, for the stories chosen drive home to us the person of Jesus so we come to feel that we really know him. This indicates that personal language statements and historical statements have much in common. Since the real self of a person is revealed through his "word," we must know something of his history in order to know him.

As Boas points out, reason has trouble with individuals because reason aims always to make universal and timeless statements. It must operate according to the law of self-consistency. A thing cannot be both *p* and not-*p*. But individuals live in time and history, and they do not behave consistently. Logic tells us that love and hate are mutually exclusive. Yet psychology finds that many mental ills arise from a person's both loving and hating another. We say that miserly and generous logically exclude each other, but, as Boas says, "We seldom ask ourselves why human beings should not be miserly in some situations and generous in others."[25] Sometimes we say of a person, with some surprise, "He is a paradox." But if we look more closely, we would not be surprised, for most men are paradoxes. The completely consistent man is an oddity, and a dull one at that.

The concept of explanation differs in the language game of personal relations from its meaning in the language of physical science. If we are asked why it is raining, the answer must be given in terms of atmospheric conditions which are the cause of the present precipitation. But, if asked why Johnny went to the store, we are not likely to respond with a physiologist's description of the neural and muscular causes of the trip. We will explain the trip in terms of purpose and will say, "He wanted to buy some candy."

In personal language, explanation must be in terms of the motives or purposes of what is to be explained. Wittgenstein says: "Why do I want to tell him about an intention, too, as well as telling him what I did?—Not because the intention was also something which was going on at that time. But because I want to tell him something about *myself,* which goes beyond what happened at that time."[26] Much confusion has arisen from the failure to see that causation belongs to a different language game from that in which we speak of purpose and intention. Of course we do speak of persons in the causal language game of science. Man is an animal in the physical universe, and there is legitimate study of man as an object of physics, chemistry, biology, and psychology. What we are saying, however, is that we cannot say all we wish to say about persons in terms of causation. We need also to use the game in which we speak of individuals as agents with motives, intentions, and purposes.

Classical discussions of the freedom of the will often have become hopelessly confused because of the failure to see that a motive is not a cause. Thus Gilbert Ryle argues that the idea that man is only a machine arises from the view that all explanation must be made in terms of the mechanical laws of the physicist. But such an idea is nonsensical. "Physicists may one day have found the answers to all physical questions, but not all questions are physical questions."[27] To illustrate, Ryle points out that the movements of billiard balls are classical examples of mechanical causation. Given knowledge of the physical properties of the table and the blow struck by the cue, we can give a completely deterministic explanation of the movements of the balls. But the laws of mechanics cannot predict or explain the course of any game of billiards. To explain that, we need to have both the rules of billiards and the various intentions and strategies of the players. Without the laws of mechanics there could be no game of billiards. Alice's game of croquet in Wonderland reveals the impossibility of skill or contest where mechanical determinism is lacking. But mechanical laws cannot explain the purpose or the development of the game. Ryle puts it: "Not only is there plenty of room for purpose where everything is governed by mechanical laws, but there would be no place for purpose if things were not so governed. Predictability is a necessary condition of planning."[28]

The confusion of causal and personal language games is increased by the fact that, as Wittgenstein saw, we use the word "why" to ask for both cause and motive.[29] Similarly, we speak so often of intentions and purposes as the "causes" of an act that we cannot say that it is grammatically wrong to do so. But it is confusing. It results in our overlooking the fact that to explain something in terms of purpose and motive is quite different from explaining it in terms of its causal history. For one thing, as Wittgenstein recognized, the finding of the cause requires a long process of examining many similar cases from out of which we arrive at a hypothesis. But we may know immediately our motive or reason for an act, and it is not a hypothesis needing verification.[30] We know the motive or the purpose of the other person when he reveals it to us, and we may believe or disbelieve him, but again it is not a hypothesis or law but knowledge or doubt about a concrete situation.

This distinction between explanation by cause and explanation by purpose is important for theological language. We have seen that it took primitive man considerable time to detect that his world consisted of things as well as selves. For the same reason it took him a long time to ask causal questions. When he asked for an explanation of the rain he looked for his answer in terms of the purpose and intentions of the gods. At a later stage man tried to explain such events in terms of "final causes." Only when science ceased to explain by purpose or final cause did it make a real advance.

But with this advance a new confusion arose. Because science is a study not of purpose but of cause, it was assumed by some that it is improper to speak of purpose at all. The ultimate absurdity arose when men appeared who tried to explain all personal actions by causal explanations alone. Applied to man, this behaviorism gave a picture such as we would have of a billiard game from a man who knew the laws of mechanics but had no idea of the rules of billiards or the strategies of billiard players.

It is a confusion of categories and language games if we say that science has made it impossible or unnecesary to speak about God's purpose for the universe. Of course science cannot tell us what is God's purpose for the universe, but it no more follows from this that He has no purpose or that it is irrelevant than it follows that the strategy of a billiard player is irrelevant because physics cannot discover it. To speak of God's purpose for the universe is to speak theologically, not scientifically. Theologians and scientists both have spoken a great deal of nonsense because they have failed to see that theology and science are two different language games, answering different questions and fulfilling different functions in life.

At one time theologians bore the major guilt, as they tried to use revelation to provide causal answers about the universe. This led to the fiasco of theologians' trying to dictate science to scientists. Theology could not hope to do anything but discredit itself in this debate. Furthermore, it is dubious whether the Bible attempts to give causal answers. Genesis does not provide a causal hypothesis to put into competition with the theory of evolution; it describes God as speaking and the earth appears (for example, Gen. 1:3). This is personal language, the language of purpose and intent, not the language of cause. What Genesis tells us is that the universe was created for the purposes of God. Thus the first chapter of John's Gospel is, for the Christian, a more complete description of creation than is Genesis.

In more recent centuries, scientists and their worshipers have been most guilty of speaking nonsense. They have argued that since science has explained everything in terms of causation, it is superstitious to ask about the purpose behind the universe. This misses Ryle's point that while physicists may one day answer all physical questions, not all questions are physical questions. Science's failure to locate purposes in the universe only demonstrates that the methods of science are not theological methods. Ultimately, to know the purpose of a man we need to have him speak his "word," through which his purpose is revealed. This is why theology, concerned with questions about the purpose of the universe, must depend upon the revealed "Word" in which God makes known his purpose.

For about a century sophisticated theology has been aware of the differing realms of science and theology. But in distinguishing between the scientific and theological realms, theology often has been perplexed to know if it could claim to have truth. Many have been prepared to admit that theology deals only with ethical values or man's existential problems, and that it says nothing about the universe, it makes no truth claims. It is practical reason, concerned with decisions, and leaves factual questions to science. No wonder the modern world finds such theology unnecessary.

But in light of the analysis of the differing language games, the time has come again for theology to put forth its truth claims. Questions of fact are not limited to science. In normal language we speak of it being a fact that the billiard player's purpose was to get his opponent into a corner. As a description of a billiard game in terms of the strategies and purposes of the players can be called factual, so can theology's discussion of God's purpose for man. Theological answers can be true or false because they are cognitive claims. Many of the recent philosophical arguments that find theological statements to be "noncognitive" or "meaningless" are based on a concept of "knowledge" which would make it impossible to speak of "knowing" our wife or friends.

APPENDIX TO CHAPTER 8

Our discussion of personal relations and language owes an obvious debt to Martin Buber. His distinction between I-it and I-thou relations has become an indispensable part of theology. There are, however, two important differences between Buber's analysis and ours. First, Buber can speak of an I-thou relation with natural objects, such as a tree.[31] He makes the valid point that there are differing ways of being related to a tree. We may come to it as botanist, lumberman, poet, or as lovers who have carved their hearts upon it. But we would argue that it is always incorrect and misleading to speak of one's relationship to a tree as I-thou, for the tree cannot make the personal response of a thou. Buber has divided all of man's relationships into two categories, I-thou and I-it. Since it is obvious that often one's relationship to a tree is not describable as I-it, it becomes necessary to describe it in terms of I-thou. Like the logical positivists, Buber fails to see that man plays more than two meaningful language games.

A second point where we distinguish our thought from Buber's is the tendency in Buber, exaggerated in some of his followers, to say that we cannot speak about the thou without falling into an I-it relationship.[32] Buber makes the point that we cannot be in a person-to-person relation when we are talking about the other person. But it is our thesis that, because man does have personal relations and knows others as persons, he can speak about these relations in the appropriate language without slipping into I-it language.

This point has implications for theology. Like Buber, many modern theologians have argued that we cannot speak "objectively" about God. Bultmann has put the point dramatically. "If by speaking 'of God' one understands *to talk 'about God,'* then such style of speaking has no sense at all."[33] To justify this claim, Bultmann says that it is as senseless to talk about God as it is to talk about love. We cannot talk about love "unless the talking about love be itself an act of love."

A psychology of love is quite different from speaking of love. Again, he argues, the relationship of fatherhood and childhood cannot be spoken about as though it were an incident in a natural relation between the individuals of a species. Reflection ruins the relationship which can only be at the point where "the father actually lives as father, the son as son."[34]

When Bultmann says that we cannot talk about love or fatherhood he is obviously making a strange use of language for, in normal speech, we do talk about love and fatherhood. What is he trying to express? The reference to psychology indicates that Bultmann is trying to get his readers to see that you cannot talk about love as you can talk about birds and bees. In other terms, Bultmann is arguing that love requires a different language game than that of natural science. But, in drawing from this valid premise the conclusion that we cannot speak about love, he is mistaken. Young people do speak about their love to their friends. But, and here Bultmann is right, they do not talk about it as a psychologist would talk about it to fellow psychologists. They speak as lovers from out of their love.

Bultmann argues that "talking about God becomes sin." Again he is using language in a strange sense. When John says that "God is love" (I John 4:16), he is, in the normal meaning of words, "speaking about God." Does Bultmann charge him with sin? Bultmann's point is that John is not writing a philosophical treatise on the nature of God, he is speaking from out of the depths of his relationship to God. There is an important difference between speaking to God and speaking about God, just as there is a difference between saying "I love you" and in telling a friend about your love. But Bultmann overlooks the fact that, as a man can tell about his love, so John, who has heard God speak to him and who has spoken to God, can speak about God. Perhaps the difference between the God of the philosophers and the God of Abraham, Isaac, and Jacob is that the philosophers' God is never known as thou and consequently is always spoken about as an "it," a hypothesis to explain the universe. But the

Biblical God is the one who has spoken and been spoken to, so that to speak about him requires a different language game.

Many theologians argue that we cannot speak about God "objectively." We need, however, to see that the terms "object" and "objective" have differing uses in different games. In empirical language an object is a "thing," an "it." We know it by "objectively" looking at it from the outside, without being involved or intimately related to it. If this were the only meaning of "objective," then we could have no objective knowledge of God, for he is not a thing but a thou.

But the term "objective" is also used to describe events that occur independently of ourselves. Thus if a girl says, "Tom loves me," it is meaningful to ask, "Is this an objective description of Tom, or is it only an expression of what the speaker would like to believe?" To raise the question of objectivity in this context is not to make Tom a thing, for things cannot love. The meaning of "objective" has a different use in personal language from its use in empirical language. Analogously we can find that there is a legitimate way to speak "objectively" of God. When John says that "God is love," we can ask whether this statement is objectively true or only an expression of John's feeling. Of course John's statement is not "objective" in the sense of a scientist's statement that "iron is metal," but there is an appropriate use of "objective" in this context.

NOTES

[1] See W. T. Blackstone, *op. cit.*, p. 66.

[2] K. Barth, *Church Dogmatics*, I.1, p. 157.

[3] P. Tillich, *Systematic Theology*, Vol. 1, pp. 244–245.

[4] S. Laeuchli, *The Language of Faith* (New York: Abingdon Press, 1962), pp. 191 ff.

[5] See Augustine, *The Trinity*, Bk 9.

[6] C. C. Richardson, "The Strange Fascination of the Ontological Argument," *Union Seminary Quarterly Review*, XVIII, No. 1 (November, 1962), 16.

[7] P. Tillich, *Theology of Culture,* p. 61.

[8] C. Kegley and R. Bretall (eds.), *Reinhold Niebuhr: His Religious, Social, and Political Thought* (New York: Macmillan Company, 1956), p. 19.

[9] G. Ryle, *The Concept of Mind* (London: Hutchinson's University Library, 1950), pp. 51–60.

[10] *Ibid.,* p. 58.

[11] S. Hampshire, *Thought and Action* (New York: Viking Press, 1960), chaps. 1, 2.

[12] *Ibid.,* p. 51.

[13] J. V. L. Casserley, *The Christian in Philosophy* (New York: Charles Scribner's Sons, 1951), p. 155.

[14] See A. J. Ayer (ed.), *Logical Positivism* (Glencoe: Free Press, 1959), p. 165 (italics are the author's).

[15] G. Ryle, *The Concept of Mind,* pp. 15 ff.

[16] L. Wittgenstein, *Philosophical Investigations,* p. 161.

[17] S. Kierkegaard, *Training in Christianity,* transl. by W. Lowrie (Princeton: Princeton University Press, 1944), pp. 197–206.

[18] J. Macmurray, *Persons in Relation* (New York: Harper & Brothers, 1961), pp. 76–85.

[19] *Ibid.,* pp. 40 ff.

[20] L. Wittgenstein, *The Blue and Brown Books,* p. 18.

[21] G. Boas, *The Limits of Reason* (New York: Harper & Brothers, 1961), p. 51.

[22] M. Mayer in *The Progressive,* Vol. 22, No. 2 (February, 1958), 26.

[23] See A. Flew (ed.), *Logic and Language,* 2d series, p. 29.

[24] A. Flew (ed.), *Essays in Conceptual Analysis,* p. 42.

[25] G. Boas, *op. cit.,* p. 26.

[26] L. Wittgenstein, *Philosophical Investigations,* p. 167.

[27] G. Ryle, *op. cit.,* p. 76.

[28] *Ibid.,* p. 81.

[29] L. Wittgenstein, *The Blue and Brown Books,* p. 15.

[30] *Loc. cit.*

[31] M. Buber, *I and Thou,* transl. by R. G. Smith (New York: Charles Scribner's Sons, 1958), pp. 6–8, 124–126.

[32] *Ibid.,* pp. 33–34.

[33] R. Bultmann, "What Sense Is There to Speak of God?" *The Christian Scholar,* XLIII, No. 3 (Fall, 1960), 213.

[34] *Ibid.,* p. 214.

9

THEOLOGICAL LANGUAGE AND PERSONAL LANGUAGE

In the last chapter we argued that when God reveals himself he reveals that the most adequate analogies for speaking about him are those drawn from personal relations. We then tried to analyze the personal language game. We are now prepared to ask how this analysis illuminates the problem of communicating the Christian faith.

It might seem that it would be easy to communicate the meaning of Christian faith if theological language overlapped personal language, for all men use personal language. And yet, ironically, this may be one of our difficulties today. We live in a depersonalizing age. Increasingly, personal relations are forced into Buber's I-it. In the rush of modern life we do not take the time necessary to come to know another person. We form many acquaintanceships but few friendships. The pressures toward conformity make it difficult to become authentically personal through decision, and then we hesitate to expose our lack of authenticity by entering into personal relations. We wear the mask that our peer group dictates and are afraid to reveal our true selves. Perhaps this is a major reason why the language of the Church sounds strange today. We see here the relevance of John's warning that if we love not our neighbor whom we have seen, we cannot love God whom we have not seen (I John 4:20).

The first thing our analysis of personal language says to Christian communication is that Christians must strive to reinstate the reality of personal knowledge and language. As Gilbert Ryle said, "men are men" is a tautology worth remembering in a day when we are tempted to think of men as machines or animals or something else.[1] Bonhoeffer saw that a renewal of theological language could come about only through prayer and service to men. We have emphasized the part that prayer and worship must play, but the New Testament also reminds us that love of God and love of our neighbor are intertwined. Perhaps we can make theological language meaningful to the world only when the Church is a place in which persons are treated as persons by persons.

The analogy with personal language enables us to see why knowledge of God depends upon revelation. In an age that worships science as the only way to knowledge, it is scandalous to speak about revelation. Typically the scientist tells us that science can have nothing to do with revelation claims. Science accepts as knowledge only what is publically demonstrable through experimentation. The scientist may welcome flashes of inspiration and may even call these "revelations," but of course they have no scientific status until they have been experimentally demonstrated in a public manner. This attitude is justified within science, and the day is long past when intelligent Christians supposed that revelation could add to scientific knowledge. However, when the scientist argues that it is impossible for him to accept revelation under any circumstances, he is refusing to recognize that there are language games beyond science.[2] In Ryle's terms, he forgets that even if physicists should answer all questions of physics, not all questions are questions of physics.

Science itself arises from a world of personal relationships, as does the whole life of man. Before a child has scientific knowledge, as Macmurray argues, he has been introduced to the paradigm of knowledge through knowing other persons. But a person is known only insofar as he reveals himself, and his revelation is received through empathetic response. If a scientist refuses to accept the knowledge of his wife or fellow workers that he can receive only through revelation, he will be a lonely and isolated individual.

All personal relations require revelation because no knowledge of persons in general can lead to knowledge of the unique person. Consequently we cannot reason from knowledge of persons in general to a knowledge of God's person. But God is not just another person; he is the Holy One, the Mystery. Unless and until he reveals himself, we cannot know who he is. This latter point reminds us that, although theological language overlaps with personal language, it is not identical with it. As Wittgenstein says, a language game has something in common with other language games, but it is not identical with any other. We can communicate our knowledge of God in personal language, but we are not speaking of a "man upstairs."

We have seen that a knowledge of persons comes primarily through their "word," which is expressed through their empirical words and acts. Similarly the Bible pictures God as acting in history and speaking through his prophets. As we would not deny that there may be real communication between persons in a nonempirical manner, so we cannot deny that there is a nonempirical way of knowing God. But the Bible is singularly free from "flashes" of illumination that come independently of historical events. The typical Biblical event of revelation includes a historical situation which is interpreted by the inspired prophet as God's "Word" to men.

We argued that in the case of personal communications we are concerned not with knowing actions as such but with knowing the self that communicates with us through the acts. Similarly, although most of the books of the Bible are either history or a commentary on history, the Bible's primary concern is not to report history. Rather, through the history the person of God is manifested. As a man's acts and words become the "word" through which he makes known his self, so the acts of God and the inspired words of the prophets become the "Word" by which God reveals his self.

We noted earlier that it was possible for men to see and hear Jesus without seeing or hearing the Word of God. Likewise, the Bible can be read as history or literature without being heard as God's revelation of his self. This is similar to personal relations. A man may say and do certain things which have one meaning to bystanders and casual friends and reveal something quite different to one who knows and loves him. Jesus said of his works and words, "He who has ears to hear, let him hear" (Mark 4:9). In personal relations also, he who wills to hear, hears what is missed by others. The words of the Bible have a different meaning for the casual reader who looks only for ancient history and literature than they have for the one who knows and loves God. Thus classical Protestantism affirmed that to hear God's Word in the Bible we need the inspiration and guidance of the Holy Spirit. That is, we must come into a personal relationship with God if we are to hear his "Word" speaking to us through the words of Scripture.

In discussing personal language we noted that in revealing his self a man does not just use his "word": he is his "word" as he truly reveals himself. Thus the Christian faith in the Bible as God's Word is rooted in the faith that Christ is the Word which is God himself (John 1:1). Christians have resisted any attempt to picture Christ as a means used by God or a mask worn by God. Christ, they have affirmed, is "Very God of Very God"; when God speaks his Word to man he is that Word which he speaks. It is unfortunate that Biblical statements about nature have been claimed to be inerrant. This is a confusion of language games. But the truth in all claims about the inerrancy of the Bible is the Christian's conviction that God truly reveals his self to man. To meet the Word of God is to meet God.

Because Christ is the Word of God, the Bible becomes the Word of God. That is, it is the record of the words and acts through which God has revealed his self to man. As the record of "God's mighty acts" it opens the way to a personal relationship with God. Hence the Bible is itself a "mighty act of God." Through history it has been the experience of Christians that when they approached the Bible seriously and listened to it, they have found not just ancient history but a living God speaking to them. When the Christian sees and hears the Word of God through the Bible his eyes are opened to the fact that God is still acting in life and history. God continues to reveal his self to those who have ears to hear.

But at this point modern man objects. He cannot accept the particularity of the Judaeo-Christian revelation. It is a scandal to him that ultimate truth should be made known to a particular people at a particular time and place and be preserved through a particular book. Isn't this unfair? Would God play favorites? Modern man is not irreligious; he is quite ready to accept a religion of logical and ethical truths that are open to all rational men, or a religion of mystical experience that is open to all seeking souls. But he finds unacceptable a religion that requires him to accept a special revelation that comes through a few events in history.

This objection of modern man is in part the result of misunderstanding. If one examines the concept of the chosen people in the Old Testament, he finds that it is not an unjust favoritism. The Jews were not chosen in order that they become favorites; they were chosen for the sake of the whole world, that all men might come to know the God of Abraham, Isaac, and Jacob (Mic. 4:2; Isa. 55:4–5). Truth was given to them only so that they might take it to all men. Far from receiving favors, they were told that more would be expected of them. They would be punished for all their sins (Amos 3:1–2). It was not an easy thing to be chosen, for the chosen people must be the suffering servant (Isa. 53). When Jesus, the chosen among the chosen, appeared, he had nowhere to lay his head, and he died on a cross. The particularism of the Bible is not that of an exclusive club, it is good news for all. The Bible is the most universalist of all books. In it the God of all men is seeking all men.

The basic problem about particularity arises, however, from thinking of all knowledge in terms of scientific knowledge. Such knowledge is regarded as open to any qualified seeker. Actually there is more particularism here than we sometimes admit. To make new discoveries one has to be qualified through a particular training, and often those not qualified not only are unable to make the discovery, they cannot understand it when it is made. Anyone who has mingled with scientists knows the jealousy they often feel over the acclaim won by the scientist lucky enough to make a discovery slightly ahead of others. But, of course, once such knowledge is discovered, it is open to all men, and logically it has no relationship to its discoverer. It is not necessary to know the personal history of Euclid and Einstein in order to understand their intellectual contributions.

But Israel was not the discoverer of truths which others might have discovered and which others can now know apart from Israel. This is so because here we are not dealing with scientific or logical language. A person is not known in terms of general truths; he is known in the concrete way in which he reveals his self in particular situations. And, as we saw in the last chapter, it is in unique situations rather than in habitual behavior that a man makes known his real self. Similarly, the Biblical God, who is truly personal, is known through his concrete and particular actions. To know God, as to know another person, we need to know a particular history.

If the essence of God were general rational and moral laws, the basic principles of the universe, then the particularity of Biblical revelation would be a rational absurdity. If the essence of God were undifferentiated being in which we lose our personalities in mystical absorption, then revelation through particular historical events would be meaningless. But if God is, as the Bible presents him, essentially a person who offers a person-to-person relationship with man, the Biblical form of revelation is the only possible way that God could be known. It would be the height of irrationality to expect knowledge of God apart from his special revelation of himself.

How do we answer the question, "What is God like?" We might answer by saying that God is loving, kind, forgiving, omnipotent, and eternal. Such an answer may be meaningful but it is not very clarifying. We must ask, "How loving, how forgiving?" So the Christian tells a story of a young carpenter who was nailed to a cross on a Palestinian hillside to die for crimes that he had not committed. As he hung there he looked down on those responsible for his death and said, "Father, forgive them, for they know not what they do" (Luke 23:34). God is like that! The story alone is an adequate answer because general terms like "loving" and "forgiving" do not take on meaning until we see them incarnate in action. They are pale recollections of many acts of varying degrees. To know what it means to call a man "loving" we need concrete examples of how he expresses love in actual situations. When the Christian speaks of God as loving or forgiving, he should not allow these words to be divorced from their concrete setting in the Biblical drama. Here we find God acting in a manner that gives a whole new dimension of meaning to the word "love."

Analytical philosophy forces us to ask whether statements about God can be meaningful at all apart from special revelation. From the time of Kant it has been seen that a problem of metaphysical thought is that it takes a concept from a particular field of experience and applies it to the whole of reality. When this is done it becomes meaningless because the possibility of contrast by which it could be decided whether or not it was being used correctly is lost. For example, in human life we contrast purposeful and nonpurposeful actions so, in any particular case, we can look for evidence to verify the claim that this action is purposeful. But if we make the metaphysical statement that *everything* occurs according to the purpose of God, there is nothing with which the statement can be contrasted. Since everything that happens is called the will of God, nothing that happens can count against the assertion. (We recall Flew's point about the child dying of cancer.) Similarly, if God is equally revealing himself in everything that happens, we have no way of knowing what his purposes may be. The child dying of cancer and Jesus blessing little children are equally expressions of the will of God. Consequently the philosopher argues that there is no difference between saying that everything is the will of God and saying that nothing is the will of God.[3]

This problem haunts all attempts at natural theology. In looking to the facts available to all rational men the natural theologian is caught in the metaphysical dilemma of trying to make statements about the whole of reality where there is nothing with which they may be contrasted. The God who is known in all things is not known in any. The more that the natural theologian attempts to make his case by pointing to certain particular events, the more his thought approaches special revelation.

The believer in special revelation, however, can make meaningful statements about God because he begins from particular events. The will and purpose of God is made known by God himself in particular events in contrast to the whole of history. The Christian may still want to say that in some sense God wills all events, but he would be wiser to say that God wills something in every event. To discover what God may will in all events we need to look first to the particular events where the will of God is made known.

In Wisdom's parable of the invisible gardener the observers of the garden could not agree how to judge whether the garden revealed the purpose of a gardener. Some features of the garden seemed to say "yes," some to say "no," and some to say "maybe." To believe in the gardener or not seemed purely a matter of how one felt about the garden. But to understand special revelation we need to change the parable. The gardener once told one of the observers something of his purpose. Now, as this observer looks at the garden he can point out, dimly no doubt, how the present status of the garden bears a relation to the purpose which the gardener revealed. He cannot tell in detail why the gardener left this particular patch of weeds, but he has an idea why there will be weeds. He knows that the gardener revealed it as his will to let others help in the garden and that some of these would-be helpers have sown tares (Matt. 13:25). Consequently the garden as actually seen is not simply the garden as designed by the gardener. Without the special word of the gardener himself we could not read his purpose from the present state of the garden. Of course the skeptic will still be unconvinced; he will argue that the meeting with the gardener was an illusion, that he cannot believe the story about the gardener until he too meets him. The believer must concede that this is right; he too would not have believed on the basis of the garden alone. Even so the interpretation can no longer be dismissed as meaningless.

The most compelling reason why man reveals his self to others is love. We reveal ourselves so that we may receive the revelation of others. When we are with a person we dislike we seldom "open up" to reveal our self. When two persons dislike each other, it sometimes occurs that if one takes the initiative and reveals his self, the other will respond and hate will turn to love. This cannot be made into a law, for there is no way of compelling another into an I-thou relation. Any compulsion, even one that comes in the name of love, distorts the relation at its beginning. When we see the revelation of God in the Bible we find that this is its nature. It is God's love that moves him to make himself known to man. Its purpose is to overcome man's estrangement from God and to lead him into the personal relationship with God for which he was created. "In this is love, not that we loved God but that he loved us and sent his Son to be the expiation for our sins" (I. John 4:10).

When God offers man a personal relationship a response is necessary. It is impossible for an I-thou relationship to be unilateral. We have all had experiences of offering our selves to others only to be rejected so that no I-thou "betweenness" could develop. It is impossible to manipulate a person into an I-thou relationship, for any hint of compulsion distorts the relationship. This is true of God's revelation. To God's Grace in revelation there must be the response of human faith.

Protestant theology always has had difficulty with expressing theoretically the relationship of Grace and faith. Following the New Testament, Protestants have asserted that justification is by Grace through faith (Eph. 2:8). Man has done and will do nothing to earn or deserve it. Yet man must have faith. Does this not mean that faith is a work that man must perform to earn his salvation? If so, this is, as Dietrich Bonhoeffer called it, "cheap grace." Protestantism, it appears, wishes to purchase its grace at the cheapest possible price.

Theories of predestination have tried to respond to this problem by affirming that God gives the faith through which man is saved. If this is the case, it appears that man has become a pawn moved into salvation or damnation. How can there be a true personal relation between God and man if man has been compelled to enter it? But if faith is not a gift and predestination is denied, is not faith a cheap work that purchases salvation?

These questions are what linguistic analysis would call "puzzles." They are not problems in life; they arise when the engine of language is idling. For centuries men have accepted their salvation as the gift of God through faith. They have not been prevented by the puzzle of whether they could have faith or not unless God gave it to them, and they have not been worried that they were earning their salvation by a work of faith. Can linguistic analysis provide therapy for these puzzles?

In the first place, these puzzles arise because we tend to think of salvation as a kind of prize or reward, and then we ask whether the reward is to be given only if a man passes certain tests. To say that God will give the prize by grace sounds like giving a scholarship to a student whether he passes or not. But salvation is not a prize; it is a personal relationship between God and man. As such it is a redeeming and transforming relationship so that man becomes "whole," the person he was created to be. Such an achievement cannot be by works, for we become a person only through the grace of interpersonal relations. Babies brought up by animals have proved to be less than persons. We become persons because other persons have revealed their selves to us and awakened in us the response of personhood. Psychologists tell us that the child who is not loved suffers psychological distortion.

But the persons who awaken personhood within others are themselves distorted personalities. The parent not only awakens personhood in his child but he also passes along defects of character. His neurosis awakens neurosis, his sin awakens sin. This remains true when the child comes to the stage of rebellion against the parent. Even the rebellion is distorted because of the distortion of the parent. In this we see, perhaps, something of the mechanism of original sin.

If our distorted personhood is to be made whole, we must be confronted by one who is a true person. We must be confronted by God. This is the point of Barth's statement that it is not a question whether God is a person but whether we are. This healing can come only if a whole person offers us an I-thou relationship with himself. And this, Christianity proclaims, is what God has done in Christ. God takes the first step and bares his self to us through the life, death, and resurrection of Christ. This is the grace without which salvation is impossible. In revealing his self God makes it apparent that he is eternally willing to accept man into the I-thou relation. It cannot be offered to the "worthy," for man cannot make himself worthy or whole before he enters into the relationship. But man must respond. If he were forced into the relationship with God, it could not be an I-thou relation. No doctrine of predestination that implies compulsion can be accepted. Man's response is his faith, his turning to God with his whole self. But we must recall what was said about faith as convictional. Faith is response to a convictor, and therefore doctrines of predestination have a truth. Faith is man's response, but it is won from him by God's offering of himself. It is a gift; it could not be man's response if God had not first offered himself.

But how can man be free if his response is a conviction that comes from a convictor who overwhelms him? Perhaps our problem is with the meaning of freedom. "Freedom" is a term that comes from personal language and needs to be seen in that context. When a man falls in love it is in many ways similar to a convictional act. No man weighs the merits of several girls and then decides to fall in love with the most meritorious. On the contrary, he *falls* in love. A woman he meets convicts him that she is the only one for him; his response is won from him. In a real sense it is a gift to him. And yet what man would cavil that it was not therefore free? What better freedom is there than this? Or, to choose another illustration, a man is sad and downhearted—the world is black. He meets someone who smiles at him, not a polite smile but a smile of friendship which is a "word" that reveals the self to be friendly. And to his surprise the man finds that he is smiling back. His smile was won from him; it was a gift to him given by the one who smiled first. And yet it would be strange to deny that he had smiled freely. His response was, in the best sense of the word, a free response. In his gloom he could not have smiled truly no matter how he twisted his lips into the form of a smile. As Luther would say, his will was in bondage. But when the other smiled, he could not help but smile in return. He had been made free to smile. Grace and faith's response are of that nature. This does not solve all the dilemmas of the doctrine of grace and faith, but they cannot be solved unless, in some such fashion, we look to the paradigm experiences of the Christian that have led him to speak of the grace of God and man's faith.

In the I-thou relation we respond by revealing our selves to the one who revealed his self to us. And so an important part of man's response to God is confession. We reveal our selves to God. When the believer prays, "I am sinful and unclean," he does not suppose that he is giving God information that hitherto God lacked. He is making his response to God's offer of a personal relationship by baring his deepest self before God. Similarly, when man praises God he is not giving God new facts about God, he is revealing his attitude to God in order to participate in the I-thou encounter. The same is true in petitionary prayer. Man is not trying to tell God to do certain things which God might have overlooked; he is confessing his dependence upon God, he is expressing the fellowship between God and man in which man shares his troubles and desires with God.

The response of faith includes doing the will of God. When the philosopher hears the Christian saying that he ought to do something because it is the will of God, he normally jumps to the conclusion that this means that God is feared and that the Christian is seeking an outside authority for his ethics. But to the Christian this is the expression of the natural consequence of the I-thou relation with God. Man is drawn by his love of God to love that which God loves.

Modern ethical philosophy argues that no ethical statement can be derived from an indicative one. The theologian usually welcomes this, as it repudiates the attempt to derive ethics from science or from Kinsey reports. But many theologians object when the same principle is applied to theological statements. From the statement that "God loves man" it cannot follow that "I ought to love men." How then are theological and ethical statements related?

In the first place, ethical statements arise from interpersonal relations. Philosophy ought to examine the relationship between ethical and personal language, for, while the one does not logically entail the other, nonetheless they are deeply interwoven. Man, in his relationship to other persons, finds himself obligated. This is convictional language, for if a man is not convicted by the relationship to see obligations, it cannot be demonstrated rationally to him. A man can be frightened into fulfilling his obligations by punitive laws or shamed into fulfillment by public pressures, but none of these can make him experience a sense of oughtness.

In fact, the essence of ethical experience does not lie in the sense of obligation. Luther suggested that when a man has the sense of obligation he has already fallen into a state of sin. The truly good man does that which is good because that is above all else what he wants to do. If a young man needs to be told that he ought to kiss his girl friend goodnight, he needs a new girl friend. Family relationships at their best need little reference to obligation. When a father has to be told that it is his obligation to support his family, he has already fallen out of the relationship of love.

Our concepts of right and wrong arise because first we love and are loyal to other persons. When we are so related to another person we naturally see that it is right to treat him well, it is wrong to take advantage of him. Thus ethical experiences are unique experiences that for the most part arise from our interpersonal relations.

If this is the nature of ethical experience, we can understand how theological and ethical statements are related. Our personal relationship to God bears ethical implications. The Christian who says that he ought to do something because it is the will of God is not committing a logical fallacy, nor is he reverting to authoritarianism. He is saying that his relationship to God is of such a nature that he sees the rightness of doing that which would please God. When the I-thou relation with God burns at white heat, Luther is right, there is no sense of obligation. We want to do that which pleases God because pleasing God is that which pleases us. When we have to stop to tell ourselves that we ought to do the will of God, we are falling out of the ideal I-thou relationship with God. But even then the sense of obligation which is experienced is based upon the relationship with God. If a man has no I-thou relationship wtih God, he may be frightened into doing the will of God by being told that God will punish him here or hereafter. But this does not bring him into an ethical relationship. He does not come to see that this is to be done because it is right and good; he is only made to see that he had better do it to save himself. But when a man is related personally to God he can come to say, "Our God . . . is able to deliver us. . . . But if not . . . we will not serve your gods" (Dan. 3:17). That kind of response can arise only from the realities of a person-to-person relationship.

We can now examine more fully what is involved in speaking of the "convictional" nature of theological language. Christian faith rests on its own evidence. It carries its own power to convict men, as it has proved through history. The Christian no more believes without evidence than does the scientist or the atheist, but when he establishes his faith on the evidence, he has to do what all men do—he has to let the evidence "speak for itself." Since the Christian Gospel promises a personal relationship between God and man, it follows that only by entering into the relationship can the evidence of Christianity be found. This is what Luther meant by saying that only God can tell you that this is God speaking.

The Christian proclaims that God has revealed himself, he has spoken his Word to man. In the events of Jewish history God began the task of making himself known to man. The Jews found themselves in personal relationship with God. At first this was more I-you than I-thou, for God was seen as related to the people as a whole rather than to individuals. But, as time passed, the promise was heard that God would write his laws on their inward hearts (Jer. 31:33). Isaiah's experience in the temple is a great landmark in the movement toward a full I-thou realization (Isa. 6:1–8). This incident begins by pointing to the mystery of God, his awe-full holiness, but it ends in an I-thou encounter as Isaiah confesses his sin, receives forgiveness, and gives himself to serve God.

For the Christian the culmination of revelation comes in Christ. As Christ lived among men they became increasingly aware of his mystery. He was one who spoke with authority (Mark 1:22). That is, he had convictional power. Finally Peter confessed that Jesus was the Christ (Matt. 16:16), and Thomas, the doubter, proclaimed him, "My Lord and my God" (John 20:28). The disciples had become aware that in the presence of Christ they were brought in a new way into the presence of God. Scholars have detected different strands of theology in the New Testament, but there was only one faith—the faith that through the person of Christ they had been brought into a saving relationship with God. On this experience the Church was called into fellowship with a new experience of I-and-thou between its members because of their I-thou relation with God in Christ. Upon this experience was built the courage that went out to face dungeon, fire, and sword. Paul spoke for the Church when he said, "I know whom I have believed" (II Tim. 1:12). Here the convictional language points to the convictor.

But Christ died and the disciples returned home in dismay. God had gone out of their lives. In the midst of this despair Christ arose. The wondering disciples found that he who had brought them into fellowship with God was still with them and had not forsaken them. But Jesus was not to stay. How was the Church to live when he who had brought it the new relationship with God was gone? What happened was that Jesus' promise was fulfilled—the Holy Spirit came.

At Pentecost the Church found that God, who had communicated with it through Christ, was coming to it with a new form and power. And so the experiential basis for the Trinity was complete. God, the mystery, the unknowable Holy One, who had made himself known through the life, death, and resurrection of Christ, had come to dwell in their lives as the Holy Spirit. To the crowds at Pentecost Peter proclaimed the Gospel. First he told of the Old Testament background, with its promise, then he described the life of Jesus as the fulfillment of the promise. When the people asked what they could do, Peter replied, "Repent, and be baptized every one of you in the name of Jesus Christ for the forgiveness of your sins; and you shall receive the gift of the Holy Spirit" (Acts 2:38). Those who made the response found that the Holy Spirit came into their lives; they were in fellowship and communion with God and they had the power to live a new life.

What does this have to do with us? We have many things that the disciples did not have. We have two thousand years of Church history and have seen the faith that seemed so ridiculous among the vagabond band of fishermen in a backwoods Roman province move out to color the whole life of Western culture and dig inroads into every corner of the earth. We have a complicated heritage of theology, much of which would have sent the heads of the disciples spinning. We have a Luther who was so gripped by the Holy Spirit that, at gravest risk to himself, he stood before the amassed power and prestige of Church and State and said, "Here I stand, I can do no other, so help me God." We have Calvin, logical and unemotional, yet something gripped him and he stood like the rock of Gibraltar for the Gospel, proclaiming that he was predestined to do so. We have John Wesley, a haunted and troubled soul, who walked into the Aldersgate Meeting and found his heart "strangely warmed" and walked out a new man. We have all of these and we have an age for which A. J. Ayer spoke when he said that all language about God is nonsense. What verifies the Gospel today?

We do not verify the Christian faith by a reference to history. It is significant that Pentecost, Worms, Geneva, and Aldersgate have occurred, but this cannot be the evidence. Historical facts verify only historical statements, not theological ones. This is one of the insights of Bultmann's work. Even if we should verify beyond question that Jesus appeared to his disciples after his death, that might only be an interesting item for the Society for Psychical Research. It is a theological statement, not a historical one, when we say that *God raised* Christ from the dead.

Personal statements are verified only when we enter into a personal relation with the person about whom we make the statement. You cannot know a person as a person without making a response. And so at Pentecost when the listeners asked Peter what they must do, he told them to repent and be baptized. They had to make their response to God if they were to enter into the relationship which is the faith that forms the verifying evidence.

But how are we to know that a relationship is offered? History alone cannot verify the faith, but without history the faith cannot be verified either. Before he called the people to make their response of repentance, Peter had related to them the events of Old Testament history and the life of Jesus. If Bultmann is right in seeing that historical statements cannot verify theological statements, one wonders if Bultmann does justice to the necessary place that history has in the proclamation of the Gospel. Personal relationship with God presupposes that God has revealed himself in certain concrete events in history. Only when God has made himself concretely known can we make a response to him.

There cannot, therefore, be a verification of the Gospel until the Gospel is proclaimed. The Gospel is proclaimed in preaching, teaching, and liturgy. It is also proclaimed through the deeds of love and mercy performed by the Church in its gratitude to God. Part of the difficulty that the modern age finds in understanding the Gospel, we have said, lies in the fact that this is a depersonalized age in which I-thou relations seem strange. Consequently a Church that is true to the Gospel must offer I-thou relations to all men. The proclamation of God's love will always sound strange in a congregation that offers no hand of fellowship to the visitor. But deeds of love, mercy, and fellowship by themselves cannot bring men to Christianity apart from the proclamation of the Gospel. Good deeds can become a Word of God only when they are placed within the context of Gospel proclamation. Missionary work that tried to be simply a matter of setting up hospitals, schools, sanitation, and agriculture without proclaiming the Gospel has failed. It not only failed to win men to the Gospel, but it also failed to fill men with any burning desire to set up hospitals, schools, sanitation, and agriculture for others who needed it.

Where the Gospel is proclaimed it demands a decision. We can verify I-it statements without making any response, but we can verify personal statements only when we enter into the give-and-take of I-thou dialogue. And so, having heard that God has spoken to us, that he has invited us into fellowship with himself, we can verify that this is so only when we respond. We confess our sin and praise God; we obey his will.

What happens when we respond to God? It is the witness of Christians through the centuries that when the response is made the Gospel's promise is fulfilled, the Holy Spirit comes. To say that the Holy Spirit comes is to say that man finds himself in a personal relationship with God, a relationship in which his life is renewed (II Cor. 5:17). This relationship itself is the verification of theological statements.

In other words, one man cannot verify theological statements to another in the way in which he can verify mathematical or scientific statements. To verify a personal statement I must introduce you to the person involved and believe that in your relationship with the person you will find the statement verified. Similarly, to verify a theological statement, the Church can do no more than introduce a man to God in the faith that God can verify himself in the relationship that will then be formed. As convictional language theology has to have the confidence that its convictor has the power to convict.

Like all verifiable statements, theological statements are verified in our experience. Although the scientist talks meaningfully about atoms and electrons that he can never experience directly, he can do so because such concepts illuminate certain things that he does experience. The verification of Christian faith also is found within man's experience. But this does not imply a return to a theology of religious experience. We are not claiming that there is some kind of mystical or uniquely religious feeling that gives men this truth. William Temple once commented that religious experience is any experience of a religious man. This is a good point. The I-thou relation with God, within which the Christian claim is verified, is a relationship that penetrates the whole of life. It is not something restricted to a few mountaintop experiences of worship when one's heart sings and God seems real: it is a continuing experience through life.

The content of Christian theology is God and his acts of revelation, not religious experience. Perhaps some analogies will clarify this point. The physicist depends upon his experience of reading dials, watching experiments, and so on, to gain knowledge. If the physicist had no experiences, he would have no science, but physics is not the study of a physicist's experiences. It is the study of nature through the experience of the physicist. Love is likewise an experience of persons. Young people who believe that they are in love are often fascinated with examining and enjoying their experience of love. But when one is truly in love, although he knows it in his experience, he does not waste time examining his experience—his attention is absorbed by the one he loves.

In the same way, although God is known in man's own experience, the Christian is not one who has curvature of the spine from looking at his own experience. His experience comes as he looks away from himself to God revealed in Christ. The material for theology is not religious experience: it is God's acts in history which are incorporated in the experience of the faithful community. The experience in which we are related to God is a gestalt experience—it involves the whole man. When a young couple fall in love it is an emotionally charged experience. They want to be together continually and to experience emotions that come from their propinquity. At this stage love seems to be primarily an emotion, so that if someone says that love is a way of knowing, he is charged with thinking with his emotions. However, when a couple emerges from the first stage of emotional ecstasy they face a crisis in their relationship. When the heart no longer beats faster as hand touches hand, many feel that love itself has flown. In our culture, tutored as it is by Hollywood, many a marriage begins to fail when the honeymoon is over because love is identified with emotional upheaval. But, in fact, this is the time when love may grow in maturity and depth as the man and woman begin the exciting adventure of exploring each other's self with a depth of mutual revelation that is possible only in the marriage relationship. When this stage is reached, it is ridiculous to refer to love as an emotion. Love is now a relationship in which two persons are more and more closely drawn together in a growing knowledge of each other. It is a gestalt relationship that involves the whole of life, a relationship built upon common joys and sorrows, common goals and solving together the countless problems, big and small, of raising a family.

When love matures it is no longer properly called an emotion, if it ever was. This is not to say that emotion no longer enters into love. On the contrary, the emotions of love become deeper and richer because they are in the context of a fuller and wider relationship. The man whose "love life" consists of flitting from one emotional spree to another is a man who has never developed beyond the first stage of love. For him love still means reaping emotional thrills. But ironically, although he has remained at the emotional level, he has missed the deepest and most satisfying emotions. He has not learned the joy of living for another person and thus coming to the deepest form of knowledge of another. He does not know the glory of a faithful commitment that is "for better for worse, for richer for poorer, in sickness and in health, to love and to cherish, till death us do part."

In an analogous way the I-thou relationship with God is a

gestalt relationship. It is interwoven with the whole of a man's life. With God he shares a common task and goal, he faces life in joy or sorrow. A conversion experience, like young love, may be primarily a matter of emotion, but the developed maturity of the life of faith can no longer be called an emotion although, as with marriage, emotion by no means is left behind. In the relationship we find that our intellects are persuaded, our wills motivated, our desires redirected, our hopes raised, and the total convictional pattern of our life remade. Of course this all occurs within our experience, where else could it occur? But at the center of the stage is not our experience but God in Christ, upon whom our gaze is directed and with whom we are in fellowship.

Christian faith is an I-thou relationship with God instituted by God and responded to by man. Theology is the attempt to formulate and to criticize the language that arises from this relationship. If the use of theological statements is to be seen in terms of the life situation from which they spring, they must be referred to this "Divine-human Encounter." In light of this we can see the value and limitations of theological language. Doctrines and theology arise as man tries to understand this relationship, and they are indispensable if man is to communicate the faith to others. Without theology there is no speaking about the faith, there is no witness, no preaching of the Gospel, no prayer addressed to God, no teaching. Therefore we cannot accept theories that would distinguish sharply between the language of "religion" and the language of "theology." But it is always well to recall that theology is not itself faith; it is the product of faith and an invitation to faith.

Theology is never an end in itself; it is an instrument to the end of the I-thou relationship with God and through God with our fellowmen. Christian theology is not glorified speculation about the nature of being. It is not, like traditional metaphysics, an attempt to still man's curiosity about the whole of reality. A theological doctrine communicates when it is seen as a challenge to decision to answer yes or no to God's invitation. Speculation about the divinity-humanity of

Jesus can easily descend into metaphysical speculation about the possibilities of time and eternity, the substance of God and man, and so on. But it becomes meaningful to the man in the pew when he is brought to see that it is a challenge to him to accept Christ as the Lord of his life in his daily decisions. It is a challenge to an encounter with the mystery of God himself, an encounter in which man becomes the authentic self that he was created to be. The true end of theology is not a system of thought but worship, fellowship, and service.

In the light of this analysis we are able to summarize our response to the challenge of analytical philosophy when it asks whether we can properly speak of "knowledge" of God or whether theological statements are properly called "cognitive." When we face this question we find that the philosophers themselves admit that the terms "cognitive" and "knowledge" are used in differing senses.[4] If, with logical positivism or a more devious form thereof, we redefine "cognitive" and "knowledge" so that they apply only to scientific forms of knowledge, then obviously theological statements are neither cognitive nor knowledge. Willem Zuurdeeg suggests that we confine the use of knowledge and cognitive to what he calls "indicative" language. Such language, he argues, is "hypothetical, provisional, more or less probable, dependent on verification and impersonal." Since these characteristics do not apply to convictional language, we should not use the terms "cognitive" and "knowledge" when referring to convictions.[5]

Zuurdeeg points up a difference between "indicative" and convictional language games, but we cannot see that it advances communication or clarity to so restrict the definitions of "cognitive" and "knowledge." Following Macmurray, we have argued that the paradigm case where man learns the meaning of "know" is found in knowing other persons. It is therefore a strange move to redefine "know" so that we can no longer properly speak of knowing another person as a person. Wittgenstein should have freed us for all time from the bogeyman which tells us that, if truth is not scientific, it is not truth.

Recognizing that knowledge of persons is legitimately called knowledge, we have argued that theological statements have an analogy to personal language. Theological statements claim to be true or false. They make statements that intend to give information about God's purpose, nature, intention, and action. They are not meant to express the feelings of the speaker. We are fully justified in describing them as cognitive, for they claim to express truth. Can we go further and say that they constitute knowledge?

Before we can answer this question we must decide what it means to "know" something. Barth has defined knowledge as "that confirmation of human acquaintance with an object whereby its trueness becomes a determining factor in the existence of the man who knows."[6] At first sight this might seem an undesirably limited definition. In normal speech we have no hesitancy in saying that we know certain things that do not determine our existence. For example, although we are not astronomers, we do not hesitate to say that we "know" that the sun is approximately 93 million miles from the earth. But this does not determine our life, for if the astronomers should tell us that their calculations were wrong and that the sun actually is twice that far away, the pattern of our life would not change. However, in such cases we are not likely to argue if someone says that we only "believe" such an item.

On the other hand, the objection might be made that Barth's definition is too broad. Our life is often determined by beliefs that later turn out to be wrong. At one time men could say, by Barth's definition, that they "knew" that there were witches, for their lives were determined by this belief. However, as analytical philosophers have made clear, if we restrict our use of "know" to situations where there is no possibility of being in error, we shall never be able to use the term.[7] Once we have said that we "know" something, it sounds paradoxical to concede later that we did not know it. But the only way for fallible men to protect themselves from such paradoxes is to cease using the terms "know" and "knowledge."

An illuminating discussion of the word "know" has been made by linguistic analyst J. L. Austin. The use of the word "know" is, he says, like the use of the term "promise." That is, it is a commitment and a pledge of the self. "When I say 'I know,' I *give others my word; I give others my authority for saying* that '*S* is *P*.'"[8] Thus, as Austin goes on to say, it is useless to say, "I know it is so, but I may be wrong." If the "I may be wrong" is based on some failure on my part to gain all the evidence, then I have no right to pledge myself by saying that I know. But if all I mean by the "I may be wrong" is that I am a human being and all human beings are fallible, then I have not told the hearer anything of which he was not aware. It may express commendable humility, but it adds no substance to the sentence.

In light of Austin's analysis we can see good reason for using Barth's definition. If the claim to know means that I give my pledge, I would be giving this pledge lightly if I did not restrict the claim to statements that do determine my life. Finally, when we see that the paradigm of "know" is found in our knowledge of persons, it is obvious that our lives are more decisively determined by knowledge of persons than by any knowledge that we have of things. Barth's definition seems justified.

Using Barth's definition, the convicted Christian has a right to speak of his knowledge of God. As John puts it, "Here is the test by which we can make sure that we know him: do we keep his commands?" (I John 2:3 N.E.B.). That is, knowledge is tested by whether or not it determines one's life. The Christian claims to have knowledge of God because he knows where to point to the Convictor that determines his life, and he dares to give his pledge that when others look they will be convicted. Of course, in making this claim to knowledge the Christian may be mistaken—he is no more infallible than any other man. But he does have evidence and reasons for his faith that, through history, have persuaded others. Unless we artificially redefine the word "knowledge" so that it means something drastically different from what it means in ordinary language, there is no good reason to deny the right of the Christian to speak of his knowledge of God.

NOTES

[1] G. Ryle, *op. cit.,* p. 81.

[2] For example see H. Shapley (ed.), *Science Ponders Religion,* p. 21.

[3] See D. F. Pears (ed.), *The Nature of Metaphysics,* p. 138.

[4] For example see W. T. Blackstone, *The Problem of Religious Knowledge,* pp. 51–54, 126.

[5] W. Zuurdeeg, *An Analytical Philosophy of Religion,* pp. 54–55.

[6] K. Barth, *Church Dogmatics,* I. 1, p. 226.

[7] For example see J. Hick, *Faith and Knowledge* (Ithaca: Cornell University Press, 1957), Part I.

[8] A. Flew (ed.) *Logic and Language,* 2d series, p. 144.

10

THE RELATIONSHIP OF THEOLOGY AND PHILOSOPHY

We began our study by pointing to the modern concern with communication. Christianity shares this concern because it is a faith that is commissioned to communicate itself. But, as we saw, the Church finds today that communication is often hindered by the "strangeness" of the language it uses. Faced with this problem, we looked to analytical philosophy to see whether, in its concern with language, it could help us speak to the problem of the meaning and use of theological language.

At first analytical philosophy did not seem to be helpful. It was so wedded to scientific thought forms that it discarded theological language and other nonscientific languages as nonsensical. But as we watched the growth of the movement we found that in its maturity it became less brash in outlawing the many discourses of man, including theology. But it remained obvious that this philosophy can be, at best, neutral so far as the claims of Christianity are concerned. We cannot hope to gain proofs of theological statements or content for theological belief from it. Conversation with this philosophy may help the theologian speak about his theological knowledge more precisely and cogently, but it cannot give additional theological knowledge. Because of this we have been careful to see our relation to this philosophy in terms of a "conversation."

To many Christians, however, the inability of analytical

philosophy to make a contribution to the proof or content of theology makes it irrelevant. Their general attitude is summed up by Jesus' statement, "He who is not with me is against me" (Matt. 12:30). The relationship of analytical philosophy to theology will be drastically different from the relationships of former philosophies to theology. In varying ways theology has been linked with such philosophies as Platonism, neo-Platonism, Aristotelianism, idealism, Whiteheadianism, and pragmatism. In these relationships the philosophy, as an active partner of theology, provided knowledge of God, man, and the universe. The precise relationship varied with the particular philosophies and theologies, but common to all was the belief that philosophy could add to and/or confirm theological knowledge. Such philosophies were hailed as indispensable weapons in the attempt to communicate with and persuade the unbeliever. In more recent years many theologians have formed an alliance with existentialist philosophy which differs from former philosophical-theological partnerships. But still theologians find in existentialist thought considerable content for theology's doctrine of man and questions about existence which theology must answer. From the perspective of these traditional relationships of philosophy and theology the conversation between theology and analytical philosophy seems to many theologians a waste of time.

The belief that theology has little to gain from conversing with analytical philosophy is well expressed by F. H. Cleobury and E. L. Mascall. These two authors have much in common. Both are Christians with a philosophical interest. Both doubt that Christianity can stand on revelation alone, and both attempt to lay a philosophical foundation for the Christian faith. Both men take analytical philosophy seriously and strive to treat it fairly, although for both it is a threat to Christian faith. But when the two begin to lay the philosophical foundation for Christianity, a strange difference becomes apparent.

Cleobury accepts philosophical idealism, which, he affirms, the analytical philosophers have not answered. It is not necessary, he tells us, to suppose that physical objects exist in themselves, and actually it is "systematically misleading" to do so, for physical objects never are knowable apart from human perception. When we change all sentences with material objects as their subjects into sentences about our experiences and actions it leaves our environment and action unchanged.[1] On the other hand, it is necessary that we accept the reality of other persons for, knowing ourselves to exist as persons, we cannot doubt the existence of others. To account for our perceptual experience we do not need the theory of material things existing in themselves. We need only to suppose that there exists objectively the mind of God, which is the reality responsible for our perceptions. By this method Cleobury believes that he can demonstrate that God exists for all except those who do "not want to be convinced."[2]

On the other hand, Mascall explicitly rejects idealism.[3] He holds to a realism that is a modified Thomistic Aristotelianism. He claims that the intellect actually grasps the reality of the object that is perceived. Normally we perceive objects through our senses, but the intellect sees through the perceptions to the reality of the existing object. The reality of the object is not something deduced from the sensible phenomena, but it is "grasped through them." To achieve this we must enter into an involved contemplation of the intelligible depths of the things.[4] Only when we accept this viewpoint is it possible for us to apprehend the finite things in such a way that we can see their dependence upon the creative activity of God.

Each of these men argues that only his method can escape the solipsism into which they believe analytical philosophy falls. Each asserts that his method is necessary to give man a confidence in his knowledge, in his world, and in his God. It is obvious that their philosophical systems give the authors a sense of security both as men and as Christians. And yet, ironically, their systems are mutually exclusive.

For Cleobury the material things of the world do not need to be thought of as existing in themselves. Science is a "fiction," not in the sense that it is false but in the sense that it deals with the world in the sense of "as if."[5] The purpose of impersonal language as used in science is not to mirror objective reality; it is simply to achieve the practical results of forecasting sensory experiences. For such a purpose it is enough to speak "as if" the world consisted of material objects in themselves. But for Mascall it is imperative that we recognize that our intellect is not dealing with its own perceptions but is grasping actual realities that exist independently of ourselves, even though our perception of them sometimes is misleading. If we do not make such an assertion, we shall lose the material world and God. Despite these differences both men claim to have a philosophical framework for the same Christian faith.

If we should examine other natural theologies, we would find still other philosophical systems being used to establish truths about God that would afford a basis for Christianity. And, as we noted in certain Thomist writers, we often find them arguing, as do Cleobury and Mascall, that *only* their philosophy can do this. It is clear that those who claim to have a philosophical prolegomenon to the faith are no more united in their viewpoint than the kerygmatic theologians. Not only is there no rational philosophical foundation for Christianity that can persuade all "rational men," there is not even one than can persuade all "rational" Christians.

Our dialogue with linguistic analysis helps us to see why this is so. The natural theologian has a convictional basis from which he begins his thinking, just as does the kerygmatic theologian or the atheist. But the natural theologian's convictional basis is a complex one. In part, no doubt, it rests on the Christian faith, but also, in part, it rests on a particular philosophy. Thus Cleobury is convicted that the most significant fact in our knowledge of the world is that we know only through our perceptions. Mascall, on the other hand, is convicted that the most significant fact is that our intellect grasps reality as something apart from our perceptions. When either man faces someone who cannot "see" that to which he is witnessing, (that is, who is not convicted by his convictor) the remaining argument is not persuasive. Cleobury will no doubt argue that such a man does not want to be convinced, and Mascall will say that he does not have the patience and humility to contemplate reality.[6] But such protests sound strange coming from men who deny that sin has corrupted man's ability to reason his way to God.

Because the natural theologian has a complex convictional basis he has to defend convictions that are crucial to the rational proof but not to Christian faith. A few years ago it was not unusual to find liberal Protestants who seemed more concerned to defend the convictions of idealist philosophy than they were to defend Biblical convictions. Their "higher criticism" applied only to the Bible and not to idealism. In light of this the attempt of kerygmatic theology to free itself from philosophical presuppositions and to speak for Biblical convictions alone seems to have a point. No doubt, as its critics claim, it is difficult, but the effort seems worth making.

When the attempt is made to speak from the convictional basis of the Christian faith alone, analytical philosophy can be a useful tool for the clarification of thinking and for problems of communication. Furthermore, the tool of philosophical analysis can be an important means of detecting hidden convictional premises and weighing them in light of Christian convictions. It is also a useful tool with which to detect the submerged convictional bases of the critics of Christianity. In other words, in face of analytical philosophy we can recall that Jesus also said, "He that is not against us is for us" (Mark 9:40).

But this quotation forces us to face another objection to our conversation. Is analytical philosophy by its very nature against theology? From its beginnings in logical positivism to its most recent forms, analytical philosophy has been either openly hostile to or deeply suspicious of metaphysics. If the later analysts do not presume, as did logical positivists, that all metaphysics can be refuted at one stroke, nonetheless they normally act upon the assumption (and perhaps the conviction) that any metaphysical statement is the result of some logical blunder. Furthermore, it is argued by some theologians that theological language is metaphysical, by definition. Consequently these men would say that the theologian who uses analytical philosophy as a tool is hiding a viper in his breast.

The analysis that dissolves metaphysics dissolves theology at the same time.

It is difficult to discuss this objection because the term "metaphysics" is used to describe a wide variety of activities. Logical positivism had a simple, clear-cut definition of metaphysics, but no metaphysician would accept it. The problem of defining metaphysics is portrayed by a recent symposium, *Prospect for Metaphysics,* edited by Ian Ramsey. The twelve contributors are, in varying degrees, committed to metaphysics, but they have almost twelve different concepts of what metaphysics is. Ninian Smart says that metaphysics includes any attempt to give religious views of the cosmos or to give reasons for believing a revelation.[7] C. B. Daly says that the "whole meaning of metaphysics" is in the question, "Why is there any Being at all—why not far rather Nothing?"[8] D. J. B. Hawkins finds the essence of metaphysics in a discussion of "Being."[9] But Hilary Armstrong says, "The 'concept of being' is to me an empty abstraction, perhaps a pseudo-concept."[10] Illtyd Trethowan finds metaphysics to be "a reflective analysis of experience, leading to a recognition of the conscious, choosing self and of the ultimate source of the self."[11] Ian Ramsey says that all metaphysics have "shared in the desire to have an outline map of the Universe."[12] It begins to look as though it is as impossible to identify what all "metaphysics" have in common as Wittgenstein found it impossible to find what all games have in common.

In light of the varying concepts of metaphysics we cannot answer in general the question as to whether theology stands or falls with "metaphysics." But we can examine the argument of one theologian, Paul Tillich, who has argued that metaphysics, or ontology as he prefers to call it, is inevitably a part of all theology.

Tillich equates philosophy and ontology by defining philosophy as "that cognitive endeavor in which the question of being is asked."[13] Tillich prefers to call this "ontology" because the term "metaphysics" may imply that we are dealing with some other world behind the world of empirical investigation. Every man, believes Tillich, has to be an ontologist, for man is aware that he consists of both being and nonbeing. Since nonbeing threatens being, man longs to find the power of being that can save him from nonbeing. Philosophies that deny ontology contradict themselves, for every philosophy has a concept, however hidden, of reality.[14]

To Tillich it is obvious that a synthesis of ontology and Biblical religion is necessary. Every Christian must assume answers to ontological questions. He must ask, "What is the 'nothing' out of which God created the world," and the answer will be ontological. To say "Jesus Christ" is to imply an ontology about the relation of the universal Logos to Jesus. To understand the history of the Bible we must ask ontological questions about what is the nature of history and how it is related to nature. To say that "God is" is to make a dramatic statement about the nature of reality, it is ontological. Although Tillich denies that there is any one ontology that Christianity must accept, he does insist that there cannot be Christian belief or theology without ontology. Hence ontology and theology stand or fall together.

Tillich's thought is a significant attempt to prove the interdependence of ontology and theology. It could be debated by noting points where logical confusion mars the argument. For example, it seems to be a logical blunder when Tillich tells us that theologians must answer what is the "nothing" out of which God created the world?[15] The word "nothing" in the phrase "created out of nothing" has the same logical structure as the "nobody" met by the king's messenger in *Through the Looking Glass*. If we could answer what nothing *is*, it would not be nothing. If we examine the great Christian theologians who have expounded the doctrine of "creation out of nothing," it is clear that most were quite aware that they were not proposing an alternative theory about what God used when he created the world. On the contrary, they were expressing the mystery of creation. They were denying that God created the world out of himself (pantheism) or out of a recalcitrant pre-existent matter (Platonism).[16]

Tillich's argument, however, should be met by looking at

its claims as a whole. Ontology, as defined by Tillich, is the cognitive endeavor in which the question of being is asked. He says, "Everyone participates in being, and everyone experiences being when he encounters beings: persons, things, events, essences."[17] Thus Tillich makes it clear that to say that *something exists* or is real is to make a statement about the nature of "being," hence is to have an ontology. Thus a claim to know something hides an ontology for "knowing is an act which participates in being or, more precisely, in an 'ontic relation,' every analysis of the act of knowing must refer to an interpretation of being."[18] Consequently whenever we ask about the relationship of language to reality we are involved in ontology.[19]

With these definitions it is clear that Tillich has won a victory and has proved that analytical philosopher and theologian alike are engaged in ontology. When in the last two chapters we argued that we must use personal language, we were engaged, by Tillich's definition, in ontology because we were affirming the reality of selves and their relations. This showed that being was of such a nature that personal relations are real. When the Bible says that God was in Christ, it makes an ontological assertion. Tillich's victory seems complete, but what has he won? He has shown that, if we define ontology as he defines it, we are all ontologists. There is no reason for analytical philosopher or theologian to argue with Tillich. If they like his definitions, they will call themselves ontologists, and if they do not like his definitions, they will not so call themselves. Tillich cannot get rid of logical positivism by saying that he does not define "meaning" as it does, and then win his own battle with the same kind of a definitional move.[20]

But Tillich is concerned to do more than win a definitional victory. Ontology, he believes, is something more than what is implicit in every statement about reality. And so he gives a further definition of ontology. It is an inquiry into "those structures, categories, and concepts which are presupposed in the cognitive encounter with every realm of reality."[21] He says that ontology is the "basic task" and that it determines the analysis of all special forms of being. It is "first philosophy."[22] Here he implies that ontology is an intellectual discipline which is to be carried out in addition to the various sciences and which is logically prior to them. In addition to the knowledge gained by the sciences the ontologist seeks "to penetrate into the structures of being by means of the power of his cognitive function and its structures."[23] As one tries to understand what seems real he is forced to plunge deeper and deeper into different levels, and finally he must get to being itself.[24]

Tillich is using two definitions of ontology. When he strives to prove the universal necessity of ontology he defines it as that which is implied in any assertion of existence or reality. Thus, to say that a statement is ontological is to say that it speaks of reality or existence. But the second definition claims far more than this implicit ontology. It is a first philosophy, a science of being, a knowledge about "reality as a whole." It logically precedes all experience, and it dictates to our interpretation of experience. Thus Tillich's own ontology forces him to insist that God is "Being Itself" and not a being, and that God is "The Personal Itself" and not a person.[25] Kenneth Hamilton demonstrates that Tillich's ontology forces him to prejudge the nature of what is given and to find that what seems to be given is merely "preliminary" and "really something else."[26] Tillich's argument to prove that ontology is inevitable applies only to the first definition. But Tillich goes on to imply that ontology in his second definition has been shown to be equally inevitable.

The distinction between the two meanings of ontology in Tillich is illuminated by P. F. Strawson, who distinguishes between "descriptive" and "revisionary" metaphysics. Descriptive metaphysics is "content to describe the actual structure of our thought about the world, revisionary metaphysics is concerned to produce a better structure."[27] Strawson argues that descriptive metaphysics differs from philosophical analysis only in scope of generality. Since it is looking at the most general features of thought, it takes less for granted than other philosophical analyses. It has to go deeper than the simple analysis of language because it is looking for those structures of thought which are taken for granted in language and therefore cannot be found explicitly within the language forms themselves.

Tillich's first definition of ontology is close to Strawson's descriptive metaphysics. At an early age children learn to distinguish between real and imaginary cats, playmates, and other things. From such beginnings the scientific disciplines go on to develop their more sophisticated and refined analyses of reality. Tillich, in his first definition of ontology, and Strawson, in his descriptive metaphysics, are concerned to analyze the criteria involved in such distinctions.

Tillich's second definition of ontology approaches Strawson's concept of revisionary metaphysics. When children or scientists talk about real cats, they are not attempting to speak about "being"—they are just talking about cats. But when metaphysics becomes revisionary, or when ontology becomes "first philosophy," the claim is introduced that ontology, because it scientifically studies being, can find superior methods of deciding what is real. Instead of coming after the decision "This is a real cat," as does descriptive metaphysics, revisionary metaphysics as first philosophy claims that from its study of being it is able to erect superior standards to decide whether or not the cat is real. In the history of philosophy this has resulted in a number of suggestions that have been radically at odds with commonly accepted ways of deciding what is real.

This raises the question as to the meaning of the "being" that a first philosophy analyzes. In ordinary speech, to say that something "has being" is to say that it is real. One's concept of being and reality are intertwined, if not identical. We learn to use terms like "being" or "reality" only after we have learned to use terms like "exists" and "real." But it is obvious that we use these terms in quite differing ways, depending upon the activity or realm of study involved.

In normal discourse we may call "real" such things as electrons, gravity, Uncle Sam, the economic law of diminishing returns, beauty, duty, mirages (that is, the water is not real, but the mirage is), dreams, sensations, and God. It cannot be said that Pickwick is a real man, but it can be said that he is a real character in a novel as against an imaginary one about whom no novel was ever written. Being seems to be an abstraction coined to try to express what all of these realities have in common. If God is to be identified with being, it begins to look as though God is to be identified with the common denominator of cats, electrons, Uncle Sam, and Pickwick.

In light of Wittgenstein's analyses we are alerted to ask if there is any common denominator in the various uses of the words "real" and "being." For example, I can say that my watch exists and that red exists; both have being. But do they exist in the same way? If my watch were smashed and the parts scattered, I would no longer say that it exists. But what would cause us to say that red no longer exists? If all red objects were annihilated, would red still have being? What if I could still have the sensation of red when someone pressed my eyeball?[28] If we look back over our list of things called real in the last paragraph, can we claim any common denominator that is involved whenever we say that something is real and thus has being? Do we not use the terms with varying shades of meaning that bear only a family resemblance to each other?

Not only is "being" a vague abstraction, but linguistic analysis is sure that to speak of being is to run the risk of category confusion. Gilbert Ryle illustrates such a confusion by supposing a man who wants to see a university and, after being shown around, says: "But where is the University? I have seen where the members of the colleges live, where the Registrar works, where the scientists experiment and the rest. But I have not yet seen the University in which reside and work the members of your University."[29] It has to be explained to this man, notes Ryle, that the university is not some counterpart to what he has seen, but that it is a means of referring to the way in which what he has seen is organized.

Tillich can say, "Everyone experiences being when he encounters beings: persons, things, events, essences."[30] Does this not subtly lead us to expect that, since we experience being when we see a cat, we can somehow look at the being apart from the cat itself? Since we can say, "The cat is real," and any five-year-old knows what we mean, we can have a science, biology, that studies cats. Is this what leads the ontologist to suppose that we can have a science, ontology, to study the "real" as biology studies the cat? Are not all attempts to so think about "being" like the man who wants to see the university after he has been taken through its buildings and has met its faculty, students, and administration?

In every science, in the arts, in ethics, and in theology there is a concern to deal with that which is "real." So each discipline refines the criteria by which it decides what is real. But when each discipline has done its best to clarify what it means by "real" and how the real is to be distinguished from the unreal, what is left for a science of ontology to do? What has been uninvestigated? It would seem that ontology could engage only in the rather elusive task of trying to find what, if anything, the various concepts of "real" have in common. Perhaps this is why, as Kenneth Hamilton puts it, "It is only philosophical theologians who require being-itself to be counted a philosophical concept."[31]

If we examine the use of the terms "real" and "being," we find that they imply a convictional basis. To say that the cat is real is to affirm that the cat has the "power" of convicting the speaker of its reality. It also affirms a conviction that, if another will look, he will likewise be convicted. To say that "God is" is to affirm that God has the "power" of convicting man of his reality. "Descriptive metaphysics" is the attempt to find what criteria are involved in any particular convictional situation. "Revisionary metaphysics" attempts to go beyond the convictional situation. It tries to demonstrate that what convicts a man is not a true convictor, or else it tries to show that what has not convicted a man is a true convictor that ought to do so. How can such a metaphysics operate? It might try logically to persuade a man that a convictor should convict him. But this is a rational absurdity. This is to try to prove that evidence is evidence at the very point where the mark of evidence is that it is that with which we prove and not that which can be proved. The other alternative is that metaphysics is a form of witnessing to a convictor. Tillich seems to accept the latter alternative when he says that "every creative philosopher is a hidden theologian" gripped by his own "ultimate concern" or faith.[32] He approaches even closer to convictional language when he affirms that "Ontology presupposes a conversion, an opening of the eyes, a revelatory experience."[33]

But this raises a further problem about Tillich's position. He affirms that theology implies an ontology, but he insists that Christianity does not depend upon any particular ontology.[34] It is obvious that when he says this he is thinking of revisionary metaphysics, for he refers to classical metaphysicians, such as Plato, Aristotle, Cusanus, and Spinoza. If Christianity is truly indifferent to their differing systems, is this not because what they have to say is really irrelevant to Christianity? But if we speak of ontology as descriptive metaphysics and recognize, as Tillich seems to do, that it involves a convictional framework, does it not follow that Christianity does depend upon a particular ontology? The Christian faith stands or falls with certain specific statements about reality—"God was in Christ," "God is love." Insofar as Christianity makes such statements it is committed implicitly to certain ontological affirmations according to Tillich's first definition of ontology. In this case, far from being indifferent to ontology, Christianity has its own ontology to offer. R. V. Smith has suggested that to speak with analytical philosophy we need to "deontologize" theology.[35] We could agree if this means that theology renounces all claims to develop a "first philosophy." But because of the vagueness of the term "ontology" a "deontologized" theology could mean one that made no claim to speak about what is real. In this case a "deontologized" theology would have committed suicide.

Our conclusion must be that Tillich has failed to make his case that theology requires an ontology in the sense of a "first philosophy." He can demonstrate only that theology inevitably involves an implicit ontology. If, by definition, ontology is involved when the child says that "Santa Claus is not real but Daddy is," then theology is ontological when it affirms the reality of God. But, as Strawson shows, metaphysics in this sense is compatible with analytical philosophy. It is not inevitable that analytical philosophy be a viper in the breast of theology.

So far in this chapter we have faced the arguments against our conversation with analytical philosophy that are based on the failure of analytical philosophy to provide a metaphysical basis for theology. But an objection might come from the opposite direction. This would protest that we have betrayed the Christian faith by our willingness to accept any help from philosophy.

The name that will immediately leap to some minds in this connection is Karl Barth. Barth is popularly interpreted as advocating the complete divorcement of theology from philosophy. Actually this is a misconception of Barth's position. On many occasions he has insisted that theology cannot be free of philosophical influence.[36] Barth knows that the terminology and language which any theologian uses must be determined by the culture, including philosophy, within which he lives.

Barth has described his real aim in launching his theological revolt as being "to emancipate understanding, both of the Bible and things in general, from the Egyptian bondage in which one philosophy after another had tried to take control and teach us what the Holy Spirit was allowed to say. . . ."[37] That is, it is clear that Barth has been determined to see that no revisionary system of metaphysics should be allowed to dictate what a Christian may say. He goes on to confess that the road turned out to be difficult and that it had many turnings and obstacles, and that he is not sure that he has yet reached the end.

In opening a conversation with analytical philosophy we have no intention of trying to turn the clock back to a pre-Barthian reliance upon philosophy. Barth asserted the freedom of theology from philosophy when he asserted at the beginning of his *Church Dogmatics* that God's Word has the power of making itself known to man; it does not wait upon any philosophical verification.[38] Our emphasis upon the convictional nature of faith and upon the uniqueness of theological language is meant to preserve this basic freedom from the passing whims of philosophical schools. In conversing with analytical philosophy we recall that the analytical philosopher himself has offered his method as a tool for thought, not as a "first philosophy."

But here again a warning comes from Barth. He concedes that there is "an element of philosophy in all theological language," but, he asks, "Can philosophy be used merely as a tool?"[39] The question must disturb us in any conversation with philosophy. One of the tragically comical aspects of life in our technical age is the way in which man's tools become ends in themselves. The science-fiction theme of the revolt of the machines is based upon a real aspect of modern life. What begins innocently as a tool often comes to dominate its user. Similarly, a philosophy, accepted as a tool, may take over theology. This has happened too often in the history of philosophical-theological relations for us to become complacent about any conversation with analytical philosophy.

But this danger cannot be a legitimate reason for refusing to enter into conversation with philosophy. No one has taught us better than Barth that theology cannot retire to the monastery and preserve its pristine purity. Theology is the servant of the Church in its proclamation of the Word. To be a faithful servant theology must allow itself to be exposed to the world. And to be exposed to the world is to risk the danger that the world may replace the Word. Theology dare not forget this danger, nor dare it turn from the world because of it.

Early in our discussion we noted that the Tower of Babel story speaks to the communication problem of our time. Men no longer have "few words," and they find that, as they speak to each other, they cannot communicate. For the Christian there is a deep relationship between the Tower of Babel and Pentecost. At Pentecost, with the coming of the Holy Spirit, each man understood the disciples speaking in his native tongue (Acts 2:6–7). The atomization of language and meaning that sin brought to Babel is healed at Pentecost, and between the two events is the fact that the Word became flesh.

In earlier years the Incarnation was defended against the attack upon the "flesh." Gnostics, believing that the flesh was evil, affirmed that Christ did not really have a human body. Today, in the crisis of communication, we need to recall that Christ in the flesh means that Christ spoke in the language milieu of man, and that means the post-Babel milieu. As Christ redeemed the flesh of man by dwelling in it, he redeemed the language of man by speaking it. He took the language of his time in homey parable and thought form, and spoke so that men could know God. The Gnostics of today deny the ability of God to reveal himself in the everyday language of man. When theology enters into conversation with the philosophers of ordinary language, it expresses its faith that God has spoken, is speaking, and will speak in the ordinary language of man.

But, in its conversation, theology must not forget that salvation is of God. Philosopher G. J. Warnock, after describing what linguistic analysis can do, notes that this will not satisfy all men. If, he says,

> . . . there are some people who still wish to complain that philosophy does not meet their requirements, that they look up like hungry sheep and are not fed, it may perhaps be proper to ask them why philosophy *ought* to meet their requirements. Hungry sheep should not expect to be fed simply because they are looking up, for they may be looking up in the wrong direction. It is no reproach to the hedger and ditcher that he does not spend time on feeding the sheep, and the sheep in fairness should admit this.[39]

Whenever theology has expected to be fed by philosophy, it has remained hungry. The philosophers of language may help the Christian speak more clearly and forcefully for his faith. But the Christian knows that he is not fed by philosophy: he is fed by the Good Shepherd (John 10:11).

NOTES

[1] F. H. Cleobury, *Christian Rationalism and Philosophical Analysis* (London: James Clarke & Co., 1959), p. 59.

[2] *Ibid.*, p. 62.

[3] E. L. Mascall, *Words and Images*, (New York: Ronald Press Co., 1957), p. 30.

[4] *Ibid.*, pp. 70–71.

[5] F. H. Cleobury, *op. cit.*, p. 91.

[6] See Mascall, *op. cit.*, pp. 85–86; Cleobury, *op. cit.*, p. 62.

[7] I. Ramsey (ed.), *Prospect for Metaphysics*, p. 91.

[8] *Ibid.*, p. 190.

[9] *Ibid.*, p. 113.

[10] *Ibid.*, p. 107.

[11] *Ibid.*, p. 152.

[12] *Ibid.*, pp. 153–154.

[13] P. Tillich, *Biblical Religion and the Search for Ultimate Reality* (Chicago: University of Chicago Press, 1955), p. 5.

[14] *Ibid.*, pp. 17–18.

[15] *Ibid.*, pp. 73–74.

[16] See L. Gilkey, *Maker of Heaven and Earth*, pp. 51 ff.

[17] P. Tillich, *Biblical Religion and the Search for Ultimate Reality*, p. 61–62.

[18] P. Tillich, *Systematic Theology*, Vol. I, p. 19.

[19] *Ibid.*, p. 20.

[20] *Ibid.*, p. 20.

[21] *Ibid.*, p. 18.

[22] *Ibid.*, p. 163.

[23] *Ibid.*, p. 23.

[24] P. Tillich, *Biblical Religion and the Search for Ultimate Reality*, pp. 12–13.

[25] *Ibid.*, pp. 82–83.

[26] K. Hamilton, *The System and the Gospel*, (New York: Macmillan Company, 1963), p. 98.

[27] P. F. Strawson, *Individuals* (London: Methuen & Co., 1961), p. 9.

[28] See L. Wittgenstein, *The Blue and Brown Books*, p. 31.

[29] G. Ryle, *The Concept of Mind*, p. 16.

[30] P. Tillich, *Biblical Religion and the Search for Ultimate Reality*, p. 62.

[31] K. Hamilton, *op. cit.*, p. 72.

[32] P. Tillich, *Systematic Theology,* Vol. I, p. 25.

[33] P. Tillich, *Biblical Religion and the Search for Ultimate Reality,* p. 65.

[34] *Ibid.,* p. 85.

[35] R. V. Smith, "Analytical Philosophy and Religious/Theological Language," *Journal of Bible and Religion,* XXX, No. 2 (April, 1962), 107.

[36] For example see K. Barth, *Church Dogmatics,* I. 1, pp. 325–326, 434.

[37] See H. W. Bartsch (ed.), *Kerygma and Myth,* Vol. II, transl. by R. H. Fuller, (London: S.P.C.K., 1962), p. 127.

[38] K. Barth, *Church Dogmatics,* I. 1, pp. 223–226.

[39] A. J. Ayer *et al., The Revolution in Philosophy,* p. 125.

INDEX